THE GOSPEL ACCORDING TO BILLY

by

Chuck Ashman

THE GOSPEL

Other Books by Chuck Ashman

The Strange Disappearance of Jimmy Hoffa
Kissinger: The Adventures of Superkraut
The Finest Judges Money Can Buy
Connally: The Adventures of Big, Bad John
Martha: The Mouth That Roared
The People vs. Angela
The CIA-Mafia Link

with an introduction by

ACCORDING
TO
BILLY

by
Chuck Ashman

ROD McKUEN

LYLE STUART INC.   *Secaucus, N.J.*

Queries regarding rights and permissions should be
addressed to Lyle Stuart Inc., 120 Enterprise Ave.,
Secaucus, N. J. 07094.

Published by Lyle Stuart Inc. Published simultaneously
in Canada by George J. McLeod Limited, Toronto, Ont.

Manufactured in the United States of America

Library of Congress Cataloging in Publication Data
Ashman, Chuck.
The gospel according to Billy.

1. Graham, William Franklin, 1918-   I.   Title.
BV3785.G69A8   269'.2092'4 [B]   77-23027
ISBN 0-8184-0251-2

Contents

For John Piper.....

Introduction

by

ROD McKUEN

Most of the information in this remarkable book by Chuck Ashman is new to me. And while I have met Billy Graham only briefly, I must say that, even before reading it, I seldom approved of Graham's methods and double standards.

For example, his two-sided stand on the Vietnam war. Remember the night Dick Cavett questioned him about his feelings on Vietnam and the Reverend replied, "Well, there are two sides to that"? Cavett shrugged, went to a commercial, and when he returned, didn't even bother to pursue the question, since Graham obviously had no intention of replying to it, or worse, just didn't have an answer. I wonder how it's possible for Graham to maintain a close relationship with Richard Nixon after what the ex-President has dragged this nation through.

I freely admit to knowing Chuck Ashman quite well. Perhaps that gives an unfair edge to this introduction. But Graham has been a public figure for all of my adult life and I have followed his ecclesiastical escapades (as has anyone who opens a newspaper or turns on a television set) as though he were a neighbor down the block. The son of the current President publicly stated that Graham received his Doctorate of Divinity from a mail order house. If so, this mail order missionary is all the more unusual for having parlayed praying to God in public and playing golf with presidents into a multimillion-dollar business.

Chuck Ashman doesn't need me to verify his credibility. It is strong enough for CBS's "60 Minutes," the NBC and ABC news departments and nearly all of the major wire services to call on him often when they need to check out leads or pick his brain about a story they are already into.

I have great admiration for Ashman as a newsman, author, and a man who revels in research. He would rather dive into an in-depth story than settle for the surface kind of reporting that lately passes for radio, television and newspaper journalism.

Again and again in reading this volume (and I have done so from cover to cover three times now) I discovered sections that were to me almost unbelievable. Each time I researched the passages in question, I came away with positive proof that what I had read was so. I can't say I've researched all of what Ashman has written here. That would have taken the same years and months that he and his staff put into their study and effort. The book is full of insight on Graham and a remarkable behind-the-scenes look at the "Billy Whiz Bang" machine that turns out newspaper columns, paragraphs that stretch into best-selling books, television specials, movies, recordings and religious rallies on nearly every continent. Graham is a freaky phenomenon that has pulled the tent down around all other mail order media ministers and do-it-yourself revivalists. Why then has no one compiled an in-depth study of Captain Billy before? Fear? That seems to be the logical answer when one remembers that it was only the same Chuck Ashman who was unafraid to take on Henry Kissinger, as well as the Teamster hierarchy, whatever the consequences. While giving us carefully documented facts, Ashman writes with compassion, humor, and most of all, in a breezy style anyone can understand and appreciate.

Since I don't know Billy Graham, I can't dislike him. In fact, I think there are other so-called "born-again Christians" that are more dangerous. Orange-juice queen Anita Bryant has set to work to ruin the chances for the passage of the Equal Rights Amendment and has vowed that she is willing to give up everything before any kind of legislation is passed on a national or local level that would provide equal housing and job opportunities to people regardless of their sex or sexual persuasion. Probably Ms. Bryant, Mr. Graham, and their ilk are responsible for the "born-again Christians" getting such a bad rap these days. At least Reverend Ike with his flash and dash, his promises of riches right here, right now, gives his flock something tangible to believe in. If rags to riches is good enough for the shepherd, why not for his flock? Even though goodliness and Godliness, according to the Commandments (remember them?), shouldn't be based on money, marbles and chalk.

The most inconstant reader of Billy Graham's newspaper column could easily discern that, among other things, he is a religious bigot. For instance, of Transcendental Meditation, he has said: "It's evil because when you are meditating, it opens up space within you for the devil to enter." I am by no means an expert on TM but I know of no religion extant, including the Rev. Graham's, that doesn't have meditation as part of its basis—the way to free your mind for prayer.

Graham's comment would have us believe that all the monks in all the monasteries, every nun in every abbey, each Jew that goes into his synagogue or makes a pilgrimage to the Wailing Wall, and all the Far Eastern and Indian religions are *evil*. Perhaps it is a way of saying only *his* religion is the true way, though that would be contradictory since all of us have seen him in sweaty closeups on television, head raised high—not bowed, eyes closed in silent prayer.

Graham once made headlines around the world when he stated that "suspected rapists should be castrated." A week later, after an outcry from preachers and laymen everywhere, he corrected himself—but certainly not to the complete satisfaction of his critics. I am sure that whatever any sensible human being's thoughts are on rape, they would agree that the "suspect" is entitled, not only by law but certainly by any moral code, to a fair trial with evidence to prove whether he or she committed the crime.

With all his bragging and boasting concerning the many Presidents he's been close to, it's interesting that the current tenant of the White House, at least to my knowledge, has not yet invited Graham to come to Washington and become the conscience of this administration. Had he done so, the invitation would have come from this country's first "born-again Christian" President.

Or is Graham gaining wisdom with age? Perhaps he has been aware that his flair for mixing political memos with prayer meetings may put him, along with Bryant and company, in conflict with the separation of church and state. Clearly, more and more people are demanding that if the church wants to be our political saviour while morally we go down the drain, then it's time they paid taxes on their large land holdings, wholly owned banks and bank accounts, hotels, restaurants and catering businesses, and most of all their foundations and corporations which remain tax free.

I don't think the Rev. Graham should be stopped. I'm not even convinced that he himself doesn't believe what he's doing and done is righteous, albeit self-righteous; but I do think it's important to take a close look at just how this phenomenon operates and has operated— particularly if one is inclined to be a member of the Reverend's congregation. This is precisely what Chuck Ashman has done.

The Reverend may indeed be holy and a man of the cloth. But perhaps that cloth, like the Emperor's new clothes, has holes enough in it to be nonexistent. You decide, after reading the facts presented in this case history. Ashman has not put Billy Graham on trial, he has merely stated uncompromisingly what he knows about the man.

For myself, I feel a "born-again Christian" should attempt to follow Thomas à Kempis' example in *The Imitation of Christ*. I have yet to see proof that Rev. Graham does so publicly or privately.

—ROD McKUEN

1977

EDITOR'S NOTE: Poet and newspaper columnist Rod McKuen is uniquely qualified to write this introduction. He describes himself as "believing in God" and says he "wouldn't mind being saved but doesn't want to be part of someone's savings account." To that end he has researched at least a dozen religions. He considers himself a card-carrying Christian and his books, including *An Outstretched Hand* (which consists of poems, prayers and meditations), are used in churches, seminaries, and religious institutions for study around the world. Many of the poems in it were chosen by clergymen from the author's previous works.

The Preacher and the Payoff

O Lord, the sin . . .
Done for the things there's money in.
                    —JOHN MASEFIELD

You had to be there to believe it, that night of May 21, 1957. Old Madison Square Garden was really packed, all the way up to the cheap seats in the upper, upper deck. Way up there, where the altitude and the cigarette smoke were enough to make your head spin.

All the arc-light cars had been rolled out into precise position on their hanging tracks, each one carefully aimed, armed, filtered, and at the ready. On the arena's main floor, the "best" of New York mingled in a sitdown crush with "worst" of New York. Upstate farmers

13

in overalls sat elbow to elbow with fancy ladies in real furs, and hawkeyed ushers patrolled the borders of all that humanity, making damn sure no one tried to bluff or end-run his way to a better, more selective vantage point.

Crowds like that were not unusual for Madison Square Garden, for heavyweight champ Archie Moore or the Knicks, wild-West rodeos, and political rallies. Yet this massive turnout was something even the most astute promoter could not have foreseen. On this special night, the cavernous old arena was playing host to an event of the spirit, and not the flesh. It had been transformed from the home of the New York Rangers hockey team to the house of God.

The Reverend William Franklin Graham had rolled into the Big Apple with his celebrated, well-heeled World-traveling Gospel and Salvation Thrill Show, and it was strictly standing room only—an evangelists' and ticket-scalpers' dream. And with all those eyes watching him inside the Garden—and all those skeptics and critics waiting outside—Reverend Billy knew he had to pull off the best single revival of his short but already fast-rising national career.

To help guarantee good results *and* good reviews, Billy decided to do something more than just put himself in the hands of his Lord. He stacked the deck a bit in his favor by dusting off an old and honored tent-show trick. The crusaders went out and hired themselves a shill.

Now, if you've never been to a carnival, or if you have led a totally honest and unfortunately sheltered life, you probably don't even know what a shill is, even though you run into one or two almost every day.

A shill is that famous baseball player who pops up on TV commercials to tell you what a close shave he gets with a certain brand of razor blades, when in real life, he keeps his beard at bay with an electric razor.

A shill is the lady who stands next to you at a department-store vegetable-slicer demonstration and runs up to buy the first unit, then dances up and down, shouting her good fortune. She us, of course, on salary from the store.

But more to the point, a shill is that tragic, tow-headed little crippled kid who comes forth at religious revivals and, on the proper cue from the healer simultaneously finds God, tosses away his crutches, and runs outside to play shortstop. A miracle like that hits the faithful where they live, assuming they don't find out that the waif was just faking his bandy legs in return for a couple of bucks. The local press loves it, and Elmer Gantry moves on to the next town.

Of course, when Billy Graham led his entourage into Madison Square Garden in 1957, the stakes were a lot higher than they would have been at some backwater Baptist meeting in Plains, Georgia, or the like. New York City required something a lot more sensational than a simple set of tiny clubbed feet. Billy needed a shill of headline-grabbing proportions. He needed to produce an anti-Christ, to be dramatically converted at center stage, for all the doubting Thomases to see and to wonder upon.

Or as Graham's disciples remember the scene, they needed somebody to "jazz up the Crusade." Schmaltz and salvation were the diet for the faithful who would fill the seats that night. And so it was.

Through careful prearrangement, the anti-Christ shill turned out to be a tough-talking little Jewish mobster from Los Angeles, sitting in Section U on the main floor, patiently awaiting his "personal decision for Christ." It's likely many people recognized the face but

15

couldn't fit a name to it. To help them make the link, Graham-paid ushers passed the word around: "Mickey Cohen, the gangster, has come to Madison Square Garden to be saved! Great God almighty! *Mickey Cohen!*"

Yes, it was Mickey Cohen, all right, America's best-known gambler, fresh from a stint in prison and a place on the front pages of newspapers across the country. Mickey the gambler, the so-called snuffer, the womanizer, the armbuster, the all-around, full-time disciple of Satan himself. A whole lot of very bad man, packed into one very short but intimidating body. Cohen was Billy Graham's felonious ace in the hole, signed, sealed, and delivered to Jesus Christ for a fee of ten thousand dollars direct from the Billy Graham treasure chest.

To earn his payoff, all Mickey had to do was stand up at the right time and walk down to Billy's podium to receive Christ as his personal savior. A piece of cake! Another miracle of press agentry was in the making. Two dozen photographers and reporters were poised at the ready to capture it for the morning editions and the overnight news wires. Tipped off in advance, they had the best seats in the Garden, and they were ready for Mickey Cohen to hit the Sawdust Trial.

But Mickey wasn't. When the call came for sinners to stand up and be saved, the mobster slouched down in his seat and stared straight ahead—right into Billy Graham's eyes. People in Section U craned their necks, while the photographers cursed each other as they tried, in vain, to elbow their way away from the stage. A man with an unmistakable Bronx accent hollered out, "Come on, Mick. You're on, pal!"

But Cohen just sat there with a slight smile on his lips, staring ahead. The double cross was in—Mickey

Cohen had taken the payoff money and run, in front of Billy and the world.

In all those years since Mickey failed to see the light, neither Dr. Garham nor his inner-circle members have been particularly open or eager to talk about "the arrangement." But Mickey, in failing health, was more than willing to oblige with the details for history's sake. In July 1976 he told me the truth, as he lay withering away from stomach cancer in a private room at the UCLA Medical Center in Los Angeles.

Cohen told me, point-blank on tape, that the salvation gambit had been set up long before the May 21 Garden rally. It was the work of two men who whirled closely in the Graham orbit—Billy's long-time friend and aide W. C. Jones and Big Jim Vaus, Mickey's former wire-tapping expert. Vaus had given up a life of crime in 1949, when Billy Graham and a radio cowboy named Stu Hamblen converted him to Christ in Los Angeles.

"From 1949 on, Jimmy was all over me about going straight," Mickey told me. "He said Graham had changed his life, and I should meet Graham personally. So I said, 'Okay, Jimmy, bring him around sometime. I'd like to meet him.' I guess Jimmy had made me some kind of project. I mean, he really wanted me to get converted like he'd been."

In late November 1949, Big Jim and Billy showed up at Mickey's LA home—in the dark of night and on the sly. "Graham seemed like an okay kind of guy," Mickey recalled. "We talked a little while about religion, how his Crusade was goin', things like that. Jimmy asked me if I needed any money or anything. I may have borrowed a few bucks; I can't remember too clear, though."

The Fabulous Forties blended into the Fantastic

Fifties. Mickey Cohen kept getting into trouble with local and federal law; Jim Vaus kept pressing him to go with God; and Billy Graham stayed in touch. In 1951, Graham visited Mickey, during one of Cohen's several stays in the Los Angeles County Jail. "I was a real celebrity on the cellblock after that," Mickey told me.

In 1955 Cohen found himself in unaccustomed money troubles. He had just emerged from federal prison for tax evasion, and he desperately needed cash to restore his lost life-style. He fell back on an old and honored underworld income technique, accepting "loans" from friends—the kind of loans that somehow never seem to get paid back.

Among Mickey's "friends in need" in 1955 was Big Jim Vaus. Shortly after his release, Mickey sat down with Vaus for a serious discussion of the future. Along for the ride was W. C. Jones, the not-so-unofficial representative of the Billy Graham Empire. The three talked at length about the Mick's spiritual well-being and how much Billy would like to help change it for the better. "They asked me if I had ever really thought about becoming a Christian. I went along with 'em and said I would like to kick it around in my head." In return for his interest in the offer, Vaus and Jones slipped Mickey eighty-five dollars, cash on the spot.

With that modest handful of greenbacks, Mickey Cohen began walking the long path that led him directly to Madison Square Garden and his big Crusade copout. According to sworn testimony in federal court, from 1955 on Mickey could get a "loan" from the Vaus-Jones connection almost at will.

It's all right there in the transcript from tax-evasion case number 17503, United States Court of Appeals for the Ninth Circuit, Southern California District, *Meyer Harris Cohen* v. *the United States of America*, 1962.

The transcript reveals that in March 1956, Mickey accepted three thousand dollars via Jim Vaus. The money was described as another friendly "loan," to help Cohen get into the legitimate tropical-plant business.

Four months later, on July 2, another three thousand dollars found its way from Big Jim to Mickey's bank account. This time, the package included a gasoline credit card, the use of a car, and office space. The generosity was growing.

Seven months later, in February 1957, plans for the Billy Graham New York Crusade were in full swing. This time, W. C. Jones himself was handing out money to Mickey through a lawyer-intermediary named Rex Egan. At least four "loans" passed along the chain—one thousand dollars, three hundred dollars, fifty dollars, and another three hundred after that, all during one month. Jones and Vaus suddenly held a lot of IOUs in their helping hands—Mickey was into them for more than ten thousand dollars overall—and it was time to call in the markers.

In mid-April 1957, Jones and Vaus met again with their favorite charity case and told him they needed an important favor. Mickey told me what went on in that discussion: "They told me that Billy Graham's Crusade was in trouble and that it needed some pizzazz. Jimmy asked me if I would become a Christian, and I said, 'Sure, why not?' They just wanted me to jazz the meeting up a little."

In truth, Mickey never had any intention of being converted. He told me so without so much as batting an eye. "I'd played them along for years. . . . They even gave me two or three hundred bucks and a room at the Waldorf, if I'd go to New York."

It was plain and simple. Mickey had conned Big Jim and W. C. out of a lot of money—something the mobster was famous for, because when it came to collecting loose cash the Mick would promise to do most anything. Promise, but not necessarily deliver.

Even former federal prosecutor Tom Sheridan goes along with that theory. And Sheridan should know—he sent Cohen to prison when the "loans" and Mickey's tax returns didn't match up in court. During an interview in late 1976, Sheridan told me outright that he was convinced that Vaus and Jones and the people they fronted for had been set up like sheep from the very beginning.

But, why? Why did a street-smart and amoral man like Mickey Cohen sit there in the Garden and kill the geese who were laying those golden eggs? What was wrong with coming forth to fake a miraculous conversion to Christ for the benefit of the suckers and his pocketbook? The answer is as ironic as any scene from *Guys and Dolls*. Mickey *liked being Jewish*.

That's the way a famous former stripper told it to me in a television interview at deserted Hollywood Park Race Track. Liz Renay had probably been closer to Mickey Cohen than anyone else in his flamboyant world. She was his lover, sidekick, and mother confessor, all rolled into one bombshell body. Liz had been by the Mick's side when Vaus and Jones had come calling; she had seen a number of the checks they delivered, and she knew what was really going on in her man's head.

"There was just no way Mickey was going to become a Christian," Liz told me. "He was proud of being Jewish. He even wore a Star of David on his trunks, back when he was a boxer.

"When there was talk that Mickey was thinking about being converted, his family—his sister especially—got really upset. He told them not to worry, because he wasn't going to do it."

To this day, Liz Renay firmly believes that Billy Graham himself was behind the payoffs, even though people like Tom Sheridan were never able to link the preacher directly to Vaus and Jones and their two-man checkbook crusade. "I went to jail once for doing the same thing Billy Graham did," she said, "but Billy didn't."

During my last visit to Mickey Cohen, I asked the dying gangster if he thought Billy was really the man behind the money.

"I sure as hell do," he said. "I wanted to make sure that he knew about [the payoff] personally. I couldn't understand how Billy could preach Christian honesty and then okay ten grand to pull a stunt like that.

"Billy just smiled at me and told me, 'Mickey, the Bible says you can't put a price on salvation.' "

Now, Mickey Cohen was anything but a paragon of virtue, but, in his last days he was brutally honest about most things in his past. And to his dying day, he felt that the Reverend Graham should have come clean and taken the heat for rigging the "Garden miracle." As he put it to me in his best Mickey Cohen style, "The ten-thousand-dollar payoff is the goddamn truth. Billy knows it, I know it—and now *you* know it."

Mickey's epic confession about Graham's unique salvation style was witnessed and taped.

Three weeks after that hospital conversation, Mickey Cohen was dead. His old friend and partner in deception had never visited or even offered long-distance comfort to his cancer-stricken "convert."

When Mickey Cohen died, Billy Graham sent no flowers, and he was conspicuously absent from the funeral ceremonies when the little gangster passed into the custody of the Big Warden in the Sky.

The best Billy could do was to say to a reporter

(whom he tried unsuccessfully to avoid, "I was sorry to hear that he passed away. I hope he found peace."

The story of the phony Mickey Cohen setup is really the Billy Graham Story as well. It tells a lot about the reality of the man standing up there, all floodlit and fire-eyed, in the pulpit. Billy Graham is a walking, talking, carefully maneuvering contradiction—of himself and most of the things he publicly stands for.

For all his humble, country-boy good looks and his squeaky-clean public-relations image, Billy Graham is the ultimate businessman, highly skilled in the arts of street fighting. He is a master of the Madison Avenue approach, exceptionally adept at packaging an abstract concept like God and converting it into both money *and* power. And he has done it on a scale unequaled by anyone in the long and dubious history of his craft. Billy Sunday couldn't do it, because he lacked modern mass communication. Oral Roberts *can't* do it now because he lacks the Graham-style organization, not to mention the Graham connections to the American upper crust and the credibility that comes only from a "love affair" with Presidents.

In reality, there are two Billy Grahams: the one who proclaims goodness, kindness, and love with sweeping gestures of a tattered, well-worn Bible; and the one who hides in dark places behind body-guarded security fences, who plays golf with neurotic, dishonest chief executives, and who even goes along with payoffs to the Mickey Cohens of this world to guarantee a successful and lucrative front.

Billy Graham probably ranks as God's best-known moral schizophrenic. Graham and his friends must spend considerable time, money, and effort to make sure that Mr. Hyde stays at home in North Carolina while Dr. Jekyll goes apreaching.

The heart of the business is the carefully polished and constantly nurtured Billy Graham image, a world-wide sales presentation that has ballooned to legendary, though highly questionable, proportions.

The Legend Versus the Reality

The Legend of Billy Graham, as we know it today through his press flacks and "house biographers," is a colorful mixture of Horatio Alger and Sergeant York, with a few pages of Dale Carnegie's *How to Win Friends and Influence People* thrown in for good measure.

It's an often-told tale of a humble and honest North Carolina farmboy who worked hard and lifted himself out of the backwoods (with time out as a Fuller Brush salesman) to national prominence and a middle-class income. It's the saga of a promising teenage base-ball player who turned to God instead of the major leagues, thanks to the hell-fire tent preaching of Morde-cai Ham.

It's the drama of a young man falling to his knees on a deserted golf course, tearfully accepting "eternal life" from the Almighty on the eighteenth hole. It's the inspiration of a fledgling minister, preaching to the frogs and the animals along a river bank; the enterprise of a dedicated student, driving trucks to pay his way through school. And it's even the heartwarming touch of a handsome young man falling hopelessly and per-manently in love with the beautiful, dark-haired daugh-ter of a pair of China missionaries.

The Billy Graham Legend is a compelling story of the good boy who grew up to be a great man, untouched by temptation, unbowed by the cynics, and unspoiled by his own success in a noble and self-sacrificing career of good and important works.

This is part of the image Billy Graham presents to the world every time he emerges from his cocoon of privacy to go forth and do battle with Satan and his sinners. He is the picture of gracefully aging, robust moral and muscular health. He is a nonstop flurry of silver-streaked hair, evenly tanned skin, and flashing white teeth.

In the pulpit, Billy Graham seems to catch God's fire from midair and hurl it by the fistful into the audience, divinely guided shafts of gospel truth. His piercing blue eyes and clear-cut tenor-voiced words sweep over the audience like the beams from God's own lighthouse, warning of rocks ahead. When he is "on" and performing under the floodlights Billy Graham is pure charisma, making each gesture and exclamation count. Standing at center stage, Billy is to salvation what Sir Laurence Olivier is to Shakespeare: a skilled and impeccably rehearsed professional actor using every bit of skill and training to the best effect.

Off stage, Billy dons a gentler image. Though his eyes still flash and his hands still poke and jab to make points, his voice drops to a soothing baritone, oozing sincerity and Southern sweetness.

That's the expertly packaged Billy Graham we have come to know and expect since he first popped up into national view from the obscure backwaters of his first Baptist ministry in a trailer park, to a post–World War II suburb of sinners. It's the Billy Graham that Billy and his backers want us to see. It's an ad-agency composite of a man who exists on paper and television but doesn't necessarily exist in real life.

In real life, little Billy Graham was born to kind

and loving parents on a North Carolina dairy farm. He *was* considered better than average at first base on local pickup teams. But his family's own anecdotes indicate that Billy spent more time avoiding his farm chores than doing them. No major-league scout ever dropped around the Graham homestead with a bonus contract to be signed.

Those who knew him back in the Roaring Twenties and the dismal Depression years recall that Billy was an inattentive and rather lazy student with no great dedication to his books or the disciplines of a good education. He was an aimless, fun-loving, loose-running sort of kid, like so many other boys in North Carolina and everywhere else in the country. In a word, he wasn't very special.

He passed through the usual difficulties of puberty and emerged with the usual acute interest in pretty girls —an interest he maintains to this day. His budding good looks and his glib talent for flirtation made Billy the center of feminine interest rather early in his life. And it seems safe to assume that a sizable portion of his Fuller Brush sales and truck-driving income was spent on his regular dates with a string of lovely young women.

In fact, Billy may have been steered to Christ by an affair of the heart, rather than by that dubious, earth-shaking conversion on the golf course. Graham's own mother holds to the theory that her son finally got "religion on the rebound," after being jilted by a childhood sweetheart who had her cap set for some other youthful suitor.

Other discrepancies in the Billy Graham story also seem deliberate. For instance, that "Doctor" the evangelist likes to put in front of his name doesn't belong there at all. Even though his college career took him through three schools (Bob Jones College, Florida Bible

College, and Wheaton College), "Dr." Billy Graham
never earned a graduate degree. The only sheepskin he
actually ever worked for gained him a bachelor's degree
in the not-so-godly study of anthropology. Over the
intervening years, of course, his fame has brought him
scores of honorary degrees, but it has never given him
the technical right to call himself anything loftier than
just plain, "Reverend" or "Mr."

If Billy's title is questionable, his theology is downright suspect. The Graham propaganda machine takes
great care to paint him as a minister of universal appeal.
It is claimed that he can sit down among men and
women of many differing beliefs and bridge religious or
theological gaps with his basic brand of ecumenical
Christianity. In reality, his presence on the scene has
often been more divisive than healing.

As we shall learn later, Billy Graham incurred the
public and outspoken wrath of England's Archbishop of
Canterbury. The crusty old leader of the normally very
tolerant Church of England all but called Billy a self-
serving and dangerous plague in God's domain.

Even within his own Baptist ranks, the Reverend
Mr. Graham is the constant target of attacks from both
moderate and fundamentalist factions. Dr. Bob Jones
looked at the conduct and accomplishments of his
former student and was not greatly impressed.

Jones once accused Billy of "watering down his
orthodoxy to please liberals and modernists . . . leading
his converts to the gates of heaven, ushering them in,
and leaving them to find their own church thereafter."

Rather than meet the criticism from his old teacher
head-on, Billy sidestepped it neatly and modestly,
saying, "What good my ministry has done I'll never
know until I get to heaven . . . and then I may find that
some obscure preacher, working in a slum mission

somewhere, has done more to advance the Kingdom of God than I."

Bob Jones is more outspoken about that possibility. "Billy Graham has done more harm to the cause of Christ than any other so-called Christian. He has set Christianity back fifty years!"

Many other clergymen of assorted denominations have assailed Billy for his mass-market, show-business approach to his work. They say he upstages the Almighty and puts himself in the spotlight, when it should be the other way around. Even the most liberal men of God find it difficult to admire a colleague who feels compelled to spread the gospel with bumper stickers, T-shirts, and lapel buttons embossed with short prayers and full-color Graham photographs.

In the area of human rights, the Reverend Mr. Graham has exhibited an almost unfailing knack for inconsistency. He has always preached that all men and women are equal in the eyes of their Maker. And in the early 1960s, he made good on his word when he praised the nonviolence of another well-known Baptist minister, Dr. Martin Luther King. Better than that, Billy hired Howard Jones of Cleveland and Ralph Bell of Taylor University, and added them to his innermost circle of trusted aides—the first black men to hold first-string status on the Graham team.

But, it was a definite risk for Graham to take the black side in the struggle for civil rights, especially since his strength so obviously lay in rural white America. When push came to shove in the mid-sixties, when the marches turned to violence and the nightriders saddled up for their last-ditch stand, Billy Graham found the risk too great. He walked away from what could have been an important role in the "Great Crusade."

Rather than take his stand, Graham backed off to a

safe distance and advised Martin Luther King to "put on the brakes" before someone got hurt.

It is not uncommon to find Billy Graham avoiding the important and controversial issues that society insists on throwing upon his doorstep. He is, by nature, firmly planted in the middle of the road, where he has the best chance of finding the biggest available audience and, of course, the biggest cash flow.

Rocking the boat with radical views is fine for a lot of smalltime clergymen. After all, they have nothing to lose but their battles and perhaps a parish or two. But the stakes are much higher for Billy Graham, because a slip of the tongue, or the conscience, could be bad for business. And business is what Billy Graham is all about.

1

The Jeu Bu$ine$$

The fundamental evil of the world
arose from the fact that the Good
Lord has not created money enough.
— HEINRICH HEINE

The Graham Empire
If you had access to those inner-sanctum computers at the Internal Revenue Service Center in Ogden, Utah, you would find the name *Reverend William Franklin Graham* neatly stored about three-quarters of the way through the G section of the memory banks. A readout of the Reverend's computer address number would reveal the neatly-prepared tax returns of a modestly-successful minister, pulling down about twenty-five thousand dollars a year.

29

What you would not see on the print sheet would be things like a lavish "donated" home on the crest of a North Carolina mountaintop. You would not see closets bursting with expensive suede sports coats and seventy-five-dollar shoes. The limousines, the first-class hotel rooms and airline seats—none of those would seem to match up very convincingly with the income of a man who supposedly lives in the unspectacular segment of the middle-income bracket. Much of the Billy Graham life-style comes as gifts from a well-heeled cadre of friends and followers, "fat cats" with favors to ask and debts to pay. The rest of the comforts flow through the expense accounts and trust lawyers, provided in ample and effective supply in Minneapolis by the Billy Graham Evangelistic Association, the center of the Graham Empire.

The ledgers of an army of certified public account-ants reveal that Billy Graham sits at the top of a twenty-million-dollar-a-year pyramid of diverse and growing financial interests. The Billy Graham Evangelistic Asso-ciation has its own book-publishing company, a motion-picture-production company, a monthly maga-zine with a five-million-copy circulation, a syndicated radio gospel program with top-dollar rates on more than nine hundred stations, plus vast holdings in stocks, bonds, and real estate.

When Billy Graham sits down with his crusading board of directors, there is little talk of saving souls in preparation for the second coming of Christ. The resur-rection is generally postponed in favor of more pressing concerns like buying a new building in some untapped city or reducing the cost of shipping and packing books like *Peace with God*, one of several Billy Graham books, translated into more than fifty languages, available in hard cover and paperback. Sales of *Peace* are advancing toward the three million mark.

Like the man who erected it, the Billy Graham Evangelistic Association started out strictly nickel-and-dime, to handle proceeds from an early 1950 crusade in Portland, Oregon. What began as a single, ill-equipped office with overdue phone bills has grown and tax-looped its way to becoming the most heavily endowed and powerful gospel organization in the world. Grahamland is a shining model for moneymaking.

Today, the home base for the Association is a surprisingly nondescript four-story red-brick building in a working-class neighborhood next to downtown Minneapolis. It's a section of town where you wouldn't expect to find the nerve center of a multimillion-dollar enterprise of such far-reaching influence and prestige. Round about are used-car lots, seedy apartment hotels, and a gaudy, growing collection of adult-book stores and pornographic-movie theaters on property leased from the Billy Graham Evangelistic Association.

Seamy as it obviously is, the neighborhood is still a regular stop for the Minneapolis tour buses filled with out-of-town visitors eager to catch a glimpse of "the House That Billy Built" at 1300 Harmon Place.

In truth, he didn't build it at all. Standard Oil did, to serve as its regional offices until 1958. That's when Graham and his board of trustees found the need and the means to expand beyond their rented facilities and bought the building from Standard with cash on the line.

That was the beginning of a Minneapolis property-buying spree of two-million-dollar proportions, which continues even to this day. It has left Graham and his association in full ownership of an entire city block. What used to be an automobile showroom and garage across the alley is now a fully remodeled office complex, connected to the main building by an enclosed, climate-controlled walkway. Nearby are other reconverted buildings of every style and pedigree, to house everything from movie distribution to bulk-mail handling. The only non-Graham properties on the entire block are one tiny hotel and one small building adjacent to it. But chances are, their days of independence are numbered as the Association reaches out for more and more space.

Even though 1300 Harmon is the seat of his financial and organizational power, Billy Graham is seldom seen around "his" neighborhood, or even in the executive cloisters within the red-brick walls. These days, only the most important of business matters bring him to Minneapolis. Problems that directly concern him can be handled by conference phone hookups to his Montreat, North Carolina, hilltop hideaway. Other, more mundane matters are efficiently dispatched by the well-oiled machinery of the Association, under the watchful eye of George Wilson. When Billy Graham sits on the throne of the Billy Graham Evangelistic Association, you'll find Wilson close by his right hand, turning edicts into action and keeping the subjects of the realm in line.

George Wilson has been Graham's "action man" since the mid-1940s when both men found themselves tagging along, on either side of the Atlantic, with the "Youth for Christ" movement. Both were considered "comers" in those early years, learning the ropes of mass crusading at a time when the war-weary world was ready and desperate enough to be "saved" by any means available. Billy was the front man, with the ability to sway the crowds. George was the inside man, equally skilled at getting the crowds to come out in the first place, and to make sure they brought their donations with them.

Although he has never attained the heady status of his long-time friend, George Wilson has much in common with Billy Graham, over and above a piece of the Association's action. He is a minister in his own right and founder of the highly successful Northwestern Book and Bible House. And like Graham, Wilson is careful to project an image of sincerity and guarded openness, to offset expensive tastes and the creature comforts that only a well-off man can afford.

I sat down with Wilson in his Minneapolis office in a face-to-face effort to find a key to the door into Billy Graham's inner life. But surrounded by the paneling, pictures, and plaques of his own turf, Wilson took care to keep most of the locks secure.

Despite his seniority in the Association, Wilson held as close to the company line as the most aspiring, rule-following clerk in the Association's mailroom.

The success of the Graham organization, Wilson told me, was basically the will and the work of God. Billy, he said, was merely the preordained instrument of God's plans, an agent, as it were, taking only a small commission to keep body and soul together for the task at hand.

As far as divine commissions go, Wilson is definitely getting a bigger percentage of God's gross billing than Graham. According to IRS records, George enjoys a nice six-figure income each year.

Although he was quick to give Billy credit for the spiritual side of the business, Wilson was equally eager —perhaps too much so—to discredit the boss's ability as nuts-and-bolts administrator. To drive this point home, George regaled us with a "house anecdote" which several-lower echelon "insiders" have since told me is more apochryphal than accurate.

It goes something like this: In 1958, when George was handling negotiations to purchase the Standard Oil headquarters, the talks were getting down to the nitty-gritty, the anxious moment of put up or shut up.

To hear George tell it, the transaction was just too big, and he called Billy on the phone for advice. Should they buy or back off and wait for something cheaper?

Billy's response was just what you would expect from a man concerned more with the mysteries of the hereafter than with the complexities of escrows and deed transfers. "George," the Reverend supposedly said, "you know better than to ask me anything like that! I don't call you up and ask you what to preach. If you think we need that building, don't ask—just buy it!"

It's a good story, which probably explains why everyone in the Association, from Graham on down, is so happy to recount it over and over again. When Wilson ran through it for me, I remember being struck by the irony of that picture hanging behind him on his office wall—a full-color smile from another man with his own portfolio of "human-touch" advocates: Richard Milhous Nixon. George explained that Nixon's brooding brow was displayed all over Graham's headquarters, not as a political statement, but as a simple act of patriotism and a reminder of who was currently in charge. The headquarters, in this respect, was not unlike embassies, post offices, and agriculture stations. Since my visit, and since the awkward turn of events called "Watergate," the Nixon pictures have been replaced by Jimmy Carter's.

My visit to George Wilson was not solely confined to artful dodging and story telling. The package also included a guided-tour of "Salvation Central," the neighborhood nickname for the Association complex. And the tour said more about Billy Graham's corporation than weeks of verbal waltzing with his second in command.

The first thing you notice is how hard it is to get beyond the functionally nondescript lobby and up the stairs to the desk of his veteran receptionist, Norma Chaudoin. The guard at the door makes sure that only expected guests pass through to Norma and the next line of electronically monitored defenses.

Ms. Chaudoin is the "button-lady" of 1300 Harmon, and at her fingertips are the switches that must be thrown to release locked doors leading to protected areas of the building, particularly the executive offices occupied by Wilson and Graham. The "people's preacher" has an almost morbid fear of strangers and surrounds himself with security second only, some say, to that of the president of the United States.

Assuming you have made it past Norma and are safely under the wary wing of George Wilson, you are permitted to wander through the corridors and warrens of one of the most efficient business operations in the country. The Association headquarters is considered a model of modern office operation and automation, a reputation richly deserved and readily apparent, even to a totally disorganized reporter who still thinks the best way to keep notes is to write them on the backs of used envelopes.

One of the wonders of 1300 Harmon is found sprawling through the top two floors of the building— offices reserved exclusively for preparation and worldwide distribution of *Decision*, Graham's personal and league-leading gospel magazine. Born out of the wish to reach a maximum number of potential contributors and to reduce reliance on expensive broadcast time, *Deci-*

sion has become a prime-growth property for the Billy Graham Evangelistic Association.

An original staff of 3 has expanded over the years to more than 110 full-time employees working out of editorial offices in Hong Kong, Australia, Tokyo, Paris, London, and Frankfurt. Most major nonreligious magazines have to settle for something less, rather than run the risk of going broke under the weight of too many bureau expenses. But there's no talk of insolvency in the *Decision* offices, and there never has been, since the second edition went to press. The magazine is self-supporting, even though it has never accepted a single line of paid advertising. It survives and expands on a basic annual subscription rate of two dollars, multiplied quite nicely by a circulation of between five and six million.

Overseas demand for the words and deeds of Billy Graham has grown to the point where each edition is set in seven different languages. For the visually handicapped there's a special edition in Braille, at extra cost.

The *Decision* operation is the printed propaganda arm of the Association. Aside from the magazine itself, the staff is deeply involved in distributing the countless tons of pamphlets and booklets sold or given away each year by the Association. The *Decision* annex in that revamped auto showroom is piled to the ceilings with printed matter and the machinery of large-scale circulation.

To keep its facts straight, for itself as well as for outsiders, *Decision* is armed with full research and data-processing facilities. The library contains more than seven thousand theological works, with a cross-indexed section devoted to virtually everything Billy Graham has written or said, along with virtually everything ever written or said about him.

In the spirit of public relations and the need to

keep an eye on what kind of information gets disseminated, the Association usually opens this vast research file to outsiders. At any given time, about two hundred college students from around the world are calling upon the people at *Decision* to obtain raw material and assistance in preparing graduate theses about Billy Graham. This may do much to explain why so many dissertations look and sound alike, whether authored in San Salvador or Urbana, Illinois.

Although *Decision* is impressive in its scope and workload, it cannot compare with the true miracle that occurs every working day at 1300. The miracle happens in the offices set aside for handling Graham's most important link with the mass congregation he claims to serve, the U.S. mail.

During the very first year the Billy Graham Evangelistic Association set up shop in Minneapolis, it was swamped by a phenomenal 100,000 pieces of mail. Today, twenty-seven years later, the flood of cards and letters has swollen to more than 1.3 million per year—better than 25,000 every week.

Fifteen full-time clerks, backed by the very latest in mail-handling hardware, spend their eight-hour days opening the letters and segregating them into two basic categories for further processing. One pile is for just plain letters and notes, requiring response. The other, higher-priority stack is for donations from the faithful. It receives immediate attention from the workers over in Data Processing.

There, the donations are fed into computers, which determine whether they come from previous contributors or from generous newcomers to the fold. The information will be useful later on, when the Association goes on fund-raising binges and needs detailed address lists. The computers also determine how the contributors will be thanked. Those who send less than five hundred dollars get a grateful form letter. Big spenders who give more than five hundred dollars receive a "personal form letter" from Billy himself. But no matter what kind of thank-you goes out, each of them includes a full receipt, for income-tax purposes.

The average donation sent to the Minneapolis headquarters comes to about seven dollars. Considering the staggering volume of mail, that average is high, certainly more than most charities enjoy. For that reason, the Graham people get just a trifle nervous when they're asked to talk about money. No one in the organization wants the contributing public to get the impression that the Billy Graham Evangelistic Association is shaking the dollar tree. It might convince a lot of people they've given enough and that it's time to perform monetary good deeds for some other, less wealthy cause.

The flow of cash through the Minneapolis mail room amounts to mind-boggling millions, prompting more than one snoopy reporter to peek through transoms and wade through mountains of accounting books in search of someone skimming well-intended money into private pockets. But to date, the probes have fallen flat for lack of evidence. Rumors have long circulated that the Association, and Billy Graham, were spared IRS investigations because of intervention of two friendly White House Administrations, one of them Nixon's pre-Watergate regime. But efforts to confirm that story have proved as fruitless as trying to find those pennies out of place in the Association ledgers.

Non-money mail receives its own special handling. Letters addressed to the editorial staff are sent to that department for disposition; new subscriptions to *Decision* wind up in Circulation; and personal invitations

38

flow into a special office, set up to handle Graham's non-stop speaking schedule.

On the average, the Reverend is asked to take part in some kind of civic or religious function fifty times a week. They come so fast and so often that it is not uncommon for hand-selected invitations to finally filter through to Billy long after the event in question has passed into history. Another computer generally comes to the rescue in the midst of the embarrassment, with sincerely worded form letters of apology.

The electronic gadgets at the Billy Graham Evangelistic Association headquarters do a lot more than spew out letters of regret. They also serve as Graham's surrogate counselors to the masses. Thousands of people write to the evangelist each week, seeking spiritual help or a well-known shoulder to cry on. To protect himself from the impossible drudgery of even spot-checking these requests, Graham has set up a staff of men, women, and machines, all thoroughly programmed to think as he thinks.

Each letter is assessed by the human specialists, and the appropriate reply is sent along. In some cases, the problem can be resolved by merely mailing out one or two of the many Billy Graham illustrated pamphlets: sagacity and understanding in just a few thin pages, at a cost of just pennies.

But when stuffing a slick reprint into an envelope won't get the job done, the staff turns to the crusading computer for the right answers. A computer operator can sit down at a keyboard, select preprogrammed paragraphs of Billy's stock advice, and put together all the elements of perfectly coherent counseling. The variations possible are almost endless.

Once the proper stanzas are placed in appropriate

39

order, another button is pushed and the computer rat-
tles out an error-free "personal" letter, complete with
Billy's own signature—all this in just fifteen seconds.

The system works so well, in fact, that other organizations, including the Republican and Democratic parties (not to mention a horde of Madison Avenue mar-
keting experts) have beaten a path through the Graham
mailroom to pick up hints and tips.

It's no surprise that Billy Graham and his Association are by far the biggest single mail users in Minneapolis, as the postmaster there confirms. According to U.S.
Postal Service records and the tally kept by the Association, 120 million pieces of mail passed in and out of
1300 Harmon last year. Projections say it will go higher
this year and higher still next year.

And according to my tour guide George Wilson . . .
his people will be able to handle it all. They can't afford
not to.

Billy Graham and his Big Silver Screen

Among all the evangelists on the saving circuit
today, Billy Graham is clearly the most multimedia. He
has often taken public pride in the fact that his big-
money use of radio, television, live appearances, and the
printed word has enabled him to reach more people
with Christ's message than Christ ever did. Not very
modest, but true.

And since Graham markets his "product" through
every available form of communication, it is not surpris-
ing that he has gone into full-scale film production to
spread the Word even farther.

Graham's romance with moviemaking began in
1950, in a smog-choked corner of California's San Fernando Valley—Burbank, the storied home of Warner

Brothers, just a five-minute drive from Hollywood, the very heart of American cinema.

Billy's first film was a modest, twenty-five thousand-dollar production called *Mr. Texas*. It was an unsophisticated combination tearjerker and plug for contributions, geared for the church-basement-meeting set. The film tells of a fallen, wise-guy cowboy who decides to turn his back on sin and saddle up for a ride into God's hand-painted sunset, the happy result of hearing Billy Graham sermonize on the radio.

The scene is pure revivalist camp, as the prodigal cowpoke turns to the camera and says, "All my life I've been riding on the wrong trail. But I'm turning back. I'm going God's way. I think it's going to be a wonderful ride."

Not exactly Academy Award material, but an important first step toward making Billy's privately owned and operated Worldwide Pictures a leader among the world's independent specialty-film houses.

It's been twenty-seven years since *Mr. Texas* turned his spiritual horse around. Since then Worldwide has been prolific—scores of films, each with one purpose in mind: to dramatize the Billy Graham magic, to apply it to "real life" situations, and to urge the audiences, subliminally, to go home after the last credit has flickered away and make out a check. The critics have never liked Billy Graham productions. But then, who needs rave reviews when less discriminating moviegoers keep coming across with cash!

Billy himself put it in more suitably euphemistic terms when he once said, "We're not trying to be the biggest or the greatest or anything else in the movie business. But it is an important undertaking, and it's part of the biggest and greatest evangelical effort ever."

Worldwide Pictures has been an immensely successful venture, no matter what the end product looks like. Because it deals with religious topics, all contributions to the studio are totally tax deductible.

Today, the Graham studios stand bigger and better than ever along a stretch of Burbank's Buena Vista Boulevard, just a stone's throw from the Walt Disney film factory. Worldwide boasts its own Hollywood-style office building and sound-stage packed with the latest in movie-making equipment. Every square inch is big time. The people who work there are among the best the industry has to offer, and they are paid accordingly. Putting pictures on film for Billy Graham is considered "a good ride."

Unraveling the financial threads of Worldwide's fabric is predictably difficult. Like its parent, the Billy Graham Evangelistic Association, the studio keeps its vital statistics legally under wraps, safely away from the light of public exposure. But, after several months of digging, and with help from insiders, I was successful in lifting the lid from some previously undisclosed numbers, piled up during one of Worldwide's busiest years.

In 1972, the Graham studios claimed assets of $320,000, along with $1 million worth of property and land holdings, totally free from any encumbrances. But despite a declared company income of $6 million—and everything owned, free and clear—Worldwide managed to wind up 1972 breaking dead even. $6 million in, $6 million out again, and thus, no federal income taxes to be paid. The state of California did somewhat better than Washington, managing to collect $496 in taxes.

The movies produced by Graham and his organization are obviously popular, although it's difficult to determine just how popular without putting yourself in the hands of Graham's statisticians. They claim that the demand from religious, fraternal, civic, and other organizations far outstrips availability.

The Association's number men claim that just one relatively unknown film, *The Restless Ones*, has been seen in more than seventeen hundred different locations, by at least four million people. And of that total audience, they claim, three hundred thousand people were so inspired that they turned to Christ on the spot.

Conversion figures like that look impressive on paper, and the Association has a long history of turning them out by the ream as proof of Billy Graham's power to change minds and lives for the better. But as we shall learn, the Graham statistics are best taken with a healthy sprinkling of salt, because no one, not even the Good Doctor, can prove that the numbers are even remotely accurate. Just because a sinner says he's become a saint doesn't mean he really has. This characteristic of human nature applies just as much in theater seats as it does in church pews.

Holy head counts aside, the movies Billy Graham makes *are* popular with the people who feel the spiritual need, or the plain curiosity, to see them. Some of the Graham productions have even rated genuine, glittery, Hollywood-style premieres, complete with celebrities, fancy engraved programs, searchlights, and special police details provided by the best-heeled force in the Western world, the Beverly Hills Police Department.

As an example, at the 1975 opening of Worldwide's most ambitious screen effort to that date, *The Hiding Place*, the prestigious Beverly Theater was filled with eight hundred anxious and beaming first-nighters eager to see and be seen. In the ranks were a dozen or so "stars" and "personalities" with easily recognized faces, reputations, and bank accounts.

The guest list abounded with names like Julie

Harris, Joseph Campanella, Jack Carter, Rose Marie, and Arthur O'Connell. Old frazzle-headed Sam Jaffe (Gunga Din and Dr. Zorba) thrilled the rubbernecks outside the Beverly as he roared up to the front door behind the wheel of a snow-white Jeep. A few of the onlookers even recognized the face of Ethel Waters, a most talented black singer and actress who'd walked the gospel trail when Billy was just a kid shagging flyballs.

I was there too, stuffed uncomfortably into my best premiere-going suit, with pencil and curiosity at the ready for another voyage into the mysteries of Graham Country. I desperately wanted to find out why all these people were there giving their best *Gone with the Wind* hoopla treatment to a Graham corporate propaganda film.

The night of Christian festivity began in earnest around seven, when Billy shared the stage, but not the spotlight, with another "model Christian," singer Pat Boone, the same white-bucked Boone whose recollection about Secretary of Agriculture Earl Butz's bigotry cost Butz his job and helped defeat Gerald Ford.

Billy led the diamond-studded congregation through a quick prayer, and then Pat took over to guide the audience through an old-fashioned medley of all-time top Gospel hymns. For the super-well-off but non-Christian members of the gathering, Pat obliged with a few traditional Jewish songs. Most tactful for Beverly Hills.

Everything was going according to careful plan—when it happened. At 7:58 P.M. a red, white, and black-painted coffee can came bounding out from the side curtains and rolled between the feet of the faithful in the first few rows.

Within seconds, the theater filled with C. S. Micro Particle tear gas, sending Billy and his entourage off-stage to safety, while the audience was left to fend for itself.

The crowd panicked, and when it was all over, more than a dozen people had been sufficiently gassed, squashed, and stomped upon to rate a press-covered once-over in a hospital emergency room. Billy was outraged. Worldwide's president, William Brown, was nearly apoplectic, and Beverly Hills Police Chief Robert Tomaw was downright red-faced.

Rather than incur the wrath of both Billy and God, Chief Tomaw ordered his entire force to find the clues and nail the gas bomb-throwing perpetrator. All the stops were pulled, and the cops fanned out like angels of vengeance. As it often does when faced with crimes other than parking tickets, the Beverly Hills PD wound up with a manila folder, tucked away in a file cabinet, neatly marked UNSOLVED. The best Tomaw could do was blame it on the American Nazi party, because the address of the strutting but powerless local Nazi chapter had been painted on the outside of the canister.

Unsatisfying as the investigation may have been, it was probably comforting to Billy Graham in the long run. After all, it can't hurt to be attacked by the nazis.

No one ever thought—or wanted to think—that the tear gas may have been just so much publicity stunting. And no one thought about the outside chance that some devil-inspired movie critic had finally had enough and decided that the tear gas bomb was mightier than the pen.

2

Go West, Young Saint

There's gold in them thar hills!
—Anonymous California
prospector, circa 1849

The long road of life is generally rocky for most men. Sooner or later, all of us find ourselves stopped cold at the crossroads of Destiny, wondering which way to turn. Choose the wrong fork, and you stand a good chance of shuffling off into oblivion. But pick the right one, and you wind up on that path leading straight to the Promised Land of Opportunity.

In 1949, Billy Graham and his modest band of tent-show revivalists stood at their crossroad and made the decision to turn west, toward the promised land of sin and tinsel, backyard barbeques and year-round sunburns—Los Angeles. There, under the shadow of the smog-shrouded palms, Billy made his first bid for the big time, and succeeded.

At first, however, it looked very much as if the Los Angeles crusade was going to fall flat, right there at the corner of Hill and Washington Streets, in the middle of what the posters described as "the world's largest tent." For three long weeks, the turnout was only modest and press coverage consisted of tiny columns tucked away at the back near the meat-market ads.

Despite Billy's efforts to publicize himself with every fast-disappearing cent in the crusade kitty, and despite full-breasted endorsement from actress Jane Russell, it looked as if Graham was going to take an embarrassing evangelistic bath. Two months earlier in Altoona, Pennsylvania, the Graham crusade had gone bust, and it seemed that there was to be a repetition in Los Angeles.

But then, just when things seemed their darkest, God stepped into the picture and steered newspaperman Wesley Hartzell through the tent flap to Billy Graham's much-needed rescue.

Hartzell worked for one of the most influential and frightening public-opinion molders in the history of publishing, the mountain-top baron of the Hearst newspaper empire, William Randolph Hearst. Hartzell was one of Hearst's pets and had the old man's ear, so when the influential reporter sent a glowing description of the Graham crusade up to San Simeon, the result was typically Hearst.

The eighty-six-year-old publisher fired off telegrams to all his editors, coast to coast, delivering a simple, two-word order: PUFF GRAHAM!

That's all Hearst needed to say. By morning, the obedient Hearst papers were singing the broad-bannered praises of Billy Graham and vaulting him, overnight, onto the list of household words. With a single dispatch, Hearst had done for Billy what he had been unable to do for his mistress, Marion Davies. Old W. R. had finally created a major star.

Hearst's intervention wasn't the only mass-media miracle of the 1949 Los Angeles crusade. Local radio station KFWB also played a major role in turning things around and making the revival an unqualified success, instead of another dismal failure. The crucial event here was the much-talked-about "conversion" of the sinful head cowpoke of KFWB's "Cowboy Church of the Air," a genuine West Coast character named Stu Hamblen.

By his own published admission, Hamblen was a hypocrite and gold-plated phony—a hard-drinking, coarse-tongued, wayward son of a Texas Methodist preacher. Not following in his father's footsteps, Stu had made a name for himself as a rodeo champ, racehorse breeder, two-fisted gambler, dance-band leader, and composer of such country-and-Western classics as "I Won't Go Huntin' with Ya, Jake, but I'll Go Chasin' Women."

On the radio, he regularly advised young listeners to go to church on Sundays, even if he didn't. As he put it, "Do as I say, but don't do as I do!"

According to the authorized Graham biography, Hamblen would have boozed and brawled his way straight to hell if it hadn't been for Billy and the good Christian nagging of Stu's wife, Suzy. Suzy dragged the fallen cowboy to the Westwood, California, home of Henrietta Mears, to rub hors d'oeuvres with Billy and Ruth at an informal meeting of the Hollywood Christian Group for Actors. Hamblen didn't want to go but finally gave in to persistent Suzy, rather than face another in a long line of domestic squabbles.

Billy and Stu hit it off like long-lost brothers, to the surprise of everyone. In fact, the vibrations were so good between the two that Hamblen invited Billy to take advantage of his huge radio audience and plug the crusade on the air. "Come and be on my radio show," he said. "*I* can fill your tent for you!"

Since Billy was desperate for any kind of free publicity, he was more than willing to drop by KFWB's studios in Burbank to share the microphone with the self-proclaimed, dyed-in-the-wool-and-proud-of-it sinner. Hamblen enjoyed the game he was playing. He even told his listeners he'd be at front row center in the Graham tent. And he did just that. Assuming the role of penitent, he came to every meeting for a full week to bask in Billy's on-stage glow and to impress the public with his attendance and his contributions. "When the plate was passed, I would put in three bucks—or maybe ten, if someone from the [Graham] Team was watching me."

Free publicity aside, Stu Hamblen was becoming an embarrassment to Billy. Everyone who knew the cowboy knew he was using the crusade for some no-cost plugging of his own. They put Billy wise to the con, and Graham attacked with ferocity from the pulpit. With a full house looking on, the provoked preacher pointed straight at Hamblen and proclaimed, "There is somebody in this tent who is leading a double life!"

Caught with his chaps down, "Wild West" Hamblen fled to the Sierras for an unscheduled hunting trip. But after a period of boozy brooding, he vowed to return and stand up to his ungrateful preacher friend, right in the middle of his own tent.

The "showdown at Hill and Washington Streets" came on Monday night, October 17, 1949. Hamblen stormed into the revival and plopped himself right down in front of Billy, with chips on both shoulders:

"When Billy Graham got up and preached a terrific sermon, I said, 'Oh, that is a lot of malarky. He is lying.' When they took up the collection, I said, 'That is a racket!' When they sang some wonderful hymns, I said, 'That singing is lousy!' "

Billy had been forewarned by Suzy Hamblen that her ill-tempered husband was on the warpath, and the preacher was ready with another pointing finger and another accusation: "There is a person here tonight who is a phony!" Bushwacked in the open again, Hamblen blew his top. He shook a fist at Billy, and roared out of the tent for a drinking binge at the long string of bars along the "Gower Gulch" section, just off Hollywood Boulevard.

As Hamblen later told it, "I first went from one bar and then to another, but I couldn't stand the taste of the drinks they poured me. Besides, their bands were hitting sour notes!

"At last I gave up and started home, and on the way Christ spoke to me."

Hamblen said he was drunk and bewildered enough to drag Suzy out of bed and hotfoot it over to the Grahams' rented apartment to bang on the door. Standing there, Hamblen demanded that Billy pray for him, and Billy refused. "Pray for yourself and find Christ for yourself," Billy said.

By 5:00 A.M., Hamblen had done enough kneeling and breast-beating on the floor of the Graham household to pass the test. Billy finally decided to let him into God's kingdom. Hamblen recalled, "I promised I would give up all that was mean and wicked in my heart. We

51

started praying and we weren't whispering! Billy prayed. Grady Wilson prayed, Suzy prayed, and I prayed. And, as I knelt by that chair, I felt I was kneeling at the feet of Jesus. 'Lord,' I prayed, 'you're hearing a new voice this morning!' "

The Lord wasn't the only one. The very next day, Hamblen went on the radio to tell his listeners, "I've quit smoking, and I've quit drinking. Tonight, at the end of Billy's meeting, I'm going to hit the sawdust trail!"

True to his word, Hamblen came forth, along with hundreds of his devoted fans. And for the remainder of the LA crusade, he was a frequent guest on the podium, to testify in glowing terms like: "I didn't know what it was like to be a real Christian. Do you know the thrill of it all?"

Thereafter, when Hamblen wasn't haranguing his followers in the tent, he was busy giving them "the word" on KFWB. His message went far and wide throughout LA County, and on November 5, 1949, it even filtered into the mind, heart, and Buick convertible of gangland wire tapper Jim Vaus.

On that fateful afternoon, Vaus was driving north on Sepulveda Boulevard, toward the San Fernando Valley, mulling over the details of a meeting he had just had with boss Mickey Cohen. They had hatched a daring and dangerous plan to defraud Saint Louis-area bookies out of a fortune. Vaus was worried about the risk of the scheme. He flipped the dial on the car radio to KFWB. A little cowboy music would be just the thing to divert his puzzled mind.

The voice on the radio was familiar: Stu Hamblen, singing the praises of his newfound friendship with Billy Graham and Jesus Christ. "Man, what that guy won't do for publicity," Vaus muttered to himself, as he gunned the Buick across Sunset Boulevard toward the Sepulveda Pass.

Big Jim didn't pay much attention to Hamblen's nonstop testimonial until a commercial break, the likes of which no one had ever heard on Los Angeles radio before. In fact, Vaus was so astounded by it that he pulled over to the side of the road to catch every detail: "Folks, take a tip from ol' Stu Hamblen. Smoking won't do you any good at all! In fact, you might as well quit! But if you've already got the habit, smoke ———s."

Vaus couldn't believe his ears. The king of the cowboy conmen was murdering his biggest sponsor, in the name of Christ! It made Vaus so curious that the very next day he took his wife, Alice, down to Washington and Hill to find out just what kind of magic Billy Graham was pulling out of his hat.

For all his faults, Jim Vaus already knew the Gospel backward and forward. Like Stu Hamblen, he was the son of a minister. As a young man, he had even taken a half-hearted shot at Bible school. But his flare for electronics and his love for big money had steered his path away from his father's footsteps, and by the time he led Alice through the tent flaps, Big Jim had an underworld reputation and two terms in prison to his credit. He was just the right kind of sinner—the headline-grabbing kind—a perfect gift for Billy Graham's thirty-first birthday.

Vaus later recalled that he felt singled out of the crowd the very instant Billy began jumping and windmilling back and forth across the stage, dragging a clip-on microphone with him. "Something about the ease with which he moved, the flash in his eyes, the conviction of his voice, gripped me. His message wasn't new—I had heard it lots of times. What amazed me was, there weren't any jokes. It was all Bible. And I knew he was telling the truth."

Score one for Graham theatrics. And score one for Billy's on-the-spot intelligence network. Thanks to a sharp-eyed *Los Angeles Times* photographer, the preacher was alerted to Big Jim's unexpected presence. And although Billy didn't know what his celebrated visitor even looked like, he ad-libbed, hoping to hit the target.

Billy gazed at the throng and said, "There is a man in this audience who has heard this story many times before and who knows this is the decision he should make. Yet again he is saying no to God. He is hardening his heart, stiffening his neck, and he's going out of this place without Christ. And yet this may be the last opportunity God will give him to decide for Christ!"

Vaus felt like a man picked out of a police lineup. All eyes were upon him as a white-haired crusade counselor arm-locked him and dragged him toward the stage with the rest of the new converts. Without realizing why, Big Jim suddenly found himself kneeling with tears in his eyes. "I prayed, 'Lord, I believe, this time from the bottom of my heart. It's going to be almost impossible to straighten out this bewildered, tangled life of mine. But if you'll straighten it out, I'll turn it over to you, all of it.'" So much for Mickey Cohen's Saint Louis ripoff. Big Jim Vaus was suddenly out of the organized-crime business.

But he wasn't out of the national limelight, by any means. Newsmen ambushed Vaus and Alice as they left the tent. "Hey, Vaus," one photographer hollered, "you've had your picture in the paper for everything else. How about letting us shoot a couple more and tell what happened here tonight?"

By dawn the next morning, the headlines told it all: WIRETAPPER VAUS HITS SAWDUST TRAIL! Millions of Americans sat down to breakfast coffee, read the news, and wondered what the hell had suddenly come over Los Angeles. Billy Graham had hit the big time—and he intended to keep it that way.

In the midst of his California success, Billy made his first indirect contact with a man who was to become a fast, although embarrassing, friend. He was a Quaker-raised first-term Republican congressman named Richard Milhous Nixon, an upstart political rookie who had already made a name for himself as a Communist hunter, campaign knife fighter, and pretty fair rear-area U.S. Navy poker player.

Although Billy and Dick did not physically meet until 1950, the groundwork was laid at the 1949 LA crusade. Nixon's parents made it to all the rallies and told Billy how much they wished he could get together with their personal pride and joy. And though he would live to regret it, Billy promised he would look Dick up the next time he was in Washington. A year later, fate brought the two together during lunchtime in the U.S. Senate dining room.

That chance meeting over a bowl of federally funded soup was a high-water mark in American political history. It was the founding of the Billy Graham–Richard Nixon Mutual Defense and Admiration Society, an unholy alliance that has stayed together through thick and thin, triumph and humiliation. Together, Billy and Dick have stonewalled the world, because they are two peas from the same pod, on stage and off.

Both men have stood shoulder to shoulder in their day, with patriotic fervor, against the real and imagined threat of the International Communist Conspiracy. Billy approved of the number Dick did on Alger Hiss, just as he later approved of another Nixonian Red killer, Joseph McCarthy. At the peak of McCarthy's Washington witch hunt, Billy publicly thanked God for "men who, in the face of public denouncement and ridicule, go loyally on in their work exposing the pinks, the lavenders, and the Reds."

Even during Watergate, Billy Graham was a staunch public supporter of Nixon. But the San Clemente exile has removed the need for Graham to go much further out on the moral and political limb with the public and the reporters. Nixon is now more or less out of the limelight. And Billy can come and go and maintain a quiet relationship with his old friend without having to worry about explaining the odd company he keeps.

Billy still believes that Nixon is "a warm, likable human being," a tough, courageous man who "disdains expediency and compromise."

Nixon has returned the compliment, calling Billy a "major moral force" in this world, a man whom he, as president, always consulted before making any major moral decision. Looking back on the Nixon years it appears that the calls from Washington to North Carolina were few and far between.

The long relationship between Billy Graham and Dick Nixon is as fascinating as it is far-fetched. To do it justice, and perhaps explain a few hidden things about both men, a chapter will be devoted to it in the pages ahead.

The Other Presidents

Aside from his friendship with Richard Nixon, Billy Graham has spent much of his adult life collecting presidents the way a teenage girl collects Ken and Barbie dolls.

Since the end of Franklin Roosevelt's record run in office, Billy has been in and out of the White House more often than the doorman. And with one embarrassing exception, he's been treated as an honored special guest.

Billy wandered into the Rose Garden with Gerald Ford at the height of the 1976 campaign, praising the man from Michigan for his goodness, and condemning Democratic challenger Jimmy Carter for talking about sex in *Playboy* magazine.

Billy sunned himself at Key Biscayne and helped Nixon search for his golf balls when they sailed into the rough.

Billy shared the last few days of Lyndon Johnson's White House residency. He helped the war-tattered Texan pack up the mementos of power and walked him to the front door. Johnson stepped out into uneasy retirement as Nixon walked in to greet his ultimate destiny and Billy Graham, both waiting in the foyer.

The Good Reverend played with the children of John F. Kennedy and made small talk with Jacqueline while offering highly publicized but unheeded Baptist advice to a Catholic president.

And before the days of Camelot, Billy took off his shoes and toasted his feet in front of the Camp David fireplace with a Protestant soldier-turned-low-key-statesman named Ike.

That "one embarrassing exception" came at the hands of a president who refused to answer the door every time Billy came knocking—the hard-bitten Harry Truman. Harry disliked evangelists in general and Billy Graham in particular. The thirty-third president laid it quite neatly on the line in his salty memoirs. Reflecting back on his own border-state youth in Missouri, Truman said,

> *It used to be you couldn't go downtown in the evening without running into a half-dozen evangelists ranting and raving and carrying on. Some of them put on their shows in tents, or at camp meetings. And some of them just stood around on street-corners and worked up a crowd. They'd stir people up for a while, but they always got over it.*
>
> *But now, we've just got this one evangelist, this Billy Graham, and he's gone off the beam.*
>
> *He's, well, I hadn't ought to say this, he's one of those counterfeits. He claims he's the friend of all the Presidents, but he never was a friend of mine when I was President!*
>
> *I just don't go for people like that. All he's interested in is getting his name in the papers!*

Truman's assessment of Billy Graham may have been somewhat limited. After all, there are those who have talked of Billy Graham as a presidential candidate!

This, then, is the story of Billy the salesman (Fuller brushes to God), Billy the lover, Billy the politician, Billy the golfer, Billy the world traveler, Billy the businessman, Billy the philosopher, and by many critics' standards, Billy the hustler.

3

The Revised Book of Ruth

*Where you go, I will go . . . and
where you lodge, I will lodge; your
people shall be my people . . . and your
God, my God.*
> —The Book of Ruth, from
> the Old Testament.

It was the very sticky summer of 1941, and yet the world was coming unglued.

The RAF had held on to win Winston Churchill's Battle of Britain, but an undaunted Adolf Hitler was on the march eastward, pushing the Russian hordes to the very limits of their survival. France had given up the ghost. The United States remained on a loose "war alert" in the vast Pacific. Americans still believed *war* was a foreign word. And Japanese pilots made daily practice runs on mock-up targets, carefully constructed from photographs snapped on the Hawaiian island of Oahu.

It was the summer of 1941, and most Americans tried hard not to think about the horrors of another war.

The United States economy was on the move again, and the Mercury V-8 coupe was the rage of the road. Blondie was the most popular and most quoted comic strip in the Sunday funnies. Shirley Temple was beginning to swell at the chest, and Lana Turner already had. The Boston Red Sox were mighty high on a young outfielder named Ted Williams.

It was the summer of 1941, and Ruth McCue Bell had already decided that she wanted to be like her mother and father, and become a missionary to China— that is, if there were still a China left, after Japan got through with it.

Ruth Bell was born in 1920, another dark-haired and precocious daughter for Dr. and Mrs. L. Nelson Bell. The Bells were well-known in Kiangsu Province because they mixed the message of God with good medicine, and good medicine was in short supply in the China of the day. Like most missionaries of the times, Dr. and Mrs. Bell faced hardship and Asian scorn with the strength of their moral convictions and the strength of U.S. Navy 5-inch breech loaders, mounted on shallow-draft gunboats. God and gunpowder have always been a reassuring combination.

Despite their good intentions, the Bells were in the wrong place at the wrong time, selling the wrong kind of dogma. China was floundering out of her age of absolute warlords and into the era of a nationalist generalissimo named Chiang. While a large number of the Chinese millions starved, a young, back-paddy firebrand named Mao promised better times to come if only he could collect enough used Springfield rifles. In the midst of it all, thousands of white men from the West shoved their economic and military feet into the Open Door of China, hoping to gain from the chaos and confusion.

In 1920, when Ruth Bell first saw the light of day, the last thing China needed was another little round-eyed lady missionary. Instead, it needed a strong man on a white horse to lead it from the civil wars and poverty of the past, into the twentieth century.

By her own account, Ruth's childhood was reasonably happy and well adjusted. Her father raised her not only as his daughter, but as a child of China. She lived as the Chinese lived, ate what they ate, thought as they thought, and spoke as they spoke. She was so much a part of the Bells' adopted land that she was fluent in several dialects even before her infant tongue had fully mastered English.

Ruth grew lovingly close to her dedicated father, as he ministered to his small pagan parish. She was constantly by his knee, whether at the pulpit or in the clinic, to learn the missionary trade by osmosis.

As each year passed, Ruth's impish curiosity about the Presbyterian God grew to adolescent interest and finally to a burning desire. By the time she was an attractive and well-turned twenty, all doubts were gone from her mind. Ruth had decided that she wanted, more than anything else in life, to carry on the family tradition and become a self-sacrificing woman of God.

Though well educated in China and part of the time in Korea, Ruth was a long way from being properly trained for her calling. She needed the discipline and the teaching of a good solid theological school. Because such a school did not exist in Asia, and because the clouds of all-out war had grown irreversibly dark, it was time for Ruth to leave her beloved China.

It was the summer of 1941, and Ruth McCue Bell packed her bags and her Bible and headed for Wheaton, Illinois, and Billy Graham.

Then, as now, Wheaton wasn't famous for much of anything except Wheaton College, one of the better theological and small-scale liberal-arts schools in the United States. For Ruth, it was like moving to another world, several incomprehensible thousand miles from Kiangsu and smack into the middle of a corn field, just an hour and a half's drive from Chicago. It was a quantum leap from the bleeding heart of China to the self-complacent, apple-pie well-being of the American Midwest.

But Ruth faced the shock of change and her fear of the unknown with determination and the knowledge that her sister Rosy would be waiting at the Wheaton railroad station, with a few Chinese words of consolation. Rosy was already a student at Wheaton, adjusting quite nicely to a life-style of rice-free dinners, saddle shoes, and Glenn Miller music. And if Rosy could follow God's predestined American plan, then Ruth figured she could too. Wheaton College would be just a stopping place on the road back to China and back to her dream.

Although Ruth could not know it as she stood on the platform in that little Illinois town, her dream was never to be, thanks to a part-time truck driver named Billy Graham.

Billy had gone into the hauling business to pay his way through college and earn a few extra dollars. He was twenty-two and more interested in anthropology and girls than in evangelism, even though the latter was doing wonders to keep him beyond the immediate grasp of that prewar draft board back in North Carolina. He was a restless, wavy-haired, good-looking young man, with a God-given knack for preaching, if only he would put his mind to it.

But in the summer of 1941 Billy's mind was on truck driving and the young pretty girl the dean of women had sent him to pick up at the station, Rosy Bell's sister.

Thinking about pretty girls was a Billy Graham weakness in those days. If you can believe the published words of his mother, Mrs. Morrow Graham, this preoccupation almost steered her son off the path of righteousness into some other, more ungodly line of work.

"All he cared about in those days was baseball and girls," said mom. "Billy was a real ladies' man, and he was always in and out of love . . . and all he wanted to be was a professional baseball player."

This was true, so the story goes, until his childhood sweetheart, Emily Massey, jilted him. Faced with rejection of his youthful ardor, Billy decided to desert the infield and turn to God. Why he gave up baseball instead of girls was something of a mystery, even to Mrs. Graham. But God works his wonders in mysterious ways, especially when he works them through Billy Graham.

In fact, it was probably a miracle that Billy was even attending a school like Wheaton. According to his mother and his friends, Billy had spent most of his formative years avoiding the education everyone wanted him to have. He was a barely average student who once set fire to a classroom in hopes the instructor would cancel a test Billy had not prepared for. That hardly fits the Billy Graham image we see today, but it's the way things were before Ruth rolled in on the midday train.

Looking back, that first trackside encounter reads like the script from the second reel of an Andy Hardy movie, without Lewis Stone. There was Billy, the simple country boy, staring bug-eyed at Ruth, the exotic and beautiful world traveler. Billy was a picture of the thunderstruck, toe-scraping-in-the-dirt bumpkin; Ruth, the very essence of proper, seam-straight sophistication, aloof, and cool in the late-August humidity. Billy admits he was dazzled by Ruth, and Ruth admits she couldn't stand Billy or his feeble first-time flirtations.

It did not help Billy's cause when he mentioned that he was a friend of Rosy's. According to the script for the next reel, Ruth later confronted her sister, chiding her for hanging about with the likes of a pushy truck driver—especially a truck driver with a southern drawl, because well-bred daughters of missionaries were expected to keep considerably more upright and better-scrubbed company, even if they were halfway around the world from home.

Of course, true to the Andy Hardy scenario, Ruth was destined to have a change of mind and a melt of heart. The change came in the most appropriate of places, the Wheaton College Student Church, just one short week after Billy had bungled so badly on his baggage run.

Fall semester was underway, and so were the obligatory daily church services for Wheaton undergraduates. Ruth and Rosy Bell were among the many who crowded into the well-worn pews that day to endure a sermon by the brand-new student pastor: a part-time truck driver named William Franklin Graham. What he lacked in experience he made up for in evangelistic *chutzpah.*

Ruth says she remembers the day as if it were yesterday, although she cannot recall the specific words of the sermon, no matter how impressive they may have been. On that Sunday, her eyes were riveted on the young man in the pulpit, as he transformed himself, in her twenty-year-old estimation, into a new trinity: Robert Taylor, Errol Flynn, and Jesus Christ.

Ruth caught herself exchanging meaningful glances with Billy and falling hopelessly in love with him at second sight. Or so the story goes, each time friends and public-relations people ask Ruth to tell it.

For two years after that special Sunday, Ruth and Billy courted and studied together, just like so many other young couples on the Wheaton campus. It was a romantic but proper relationship, heavy on hand holding and soulful glances. As Ruth grew deeper in love and China fell further under Japanese control her dream to become a missionary began to fade. Then it all but died when her mother and father left Kiangsu and moved back to the United States and a medical practice in the very non-Chinese town of Montreat, North Carolina—Billy Graham's backyard.

While Ruth was losing missionary zeal, Billy was doing just the opposite. During that two-year courtship he knuckled down to the Bible and the other books and quit ducking out of the theology classes he had formerly avoided. Though he still majored in anthropology, he set his sights on preaching the Gospel to a parish he could call his own, in return for an income that could, one day, support a wife and family and a few extras.

With Ruth tagging along, Billy preached from every vacant pulpit he could find, and word got around that he was a vocal young man on the way up. His style grew colorful and compelling, with broad gestures and arresting blue-eyed stares. He sold his God to the borrowed congregations the way he had sold Fuller brushes to housewives, and he sold himself, forever, to Ruth.

On August 13, 1943, Ruth McCue Bell willingly put away the prospect of a return to China and married Billy Graham. The setting was a strange one for a Southern Baptist groom—a Presbyterian chapel at a Presbyterian missionary-training center. But that was what Ruth and the family wanted. The bride had no intention of giving up her denomination.

Next came a seven-day honeymoon for the Grahams at a quiet tourist lodge near Blowing Rock, North Carolina. The weather was nice, the mood was romantic, and the cost was seventy dollars. A honeymoon for just ten dollars a day was a good way to start a marriage economically—and to start the well-worn myth that Bill Graham lives modestly.

In late August 1943, Ruth and Billy were back in Illinois, he to begin a one-year apprentice-preaching assignment at the First Baptist Church of Western Springs (a Chicago suburb), she to set up chintz-curtain housekeeping and to get pregnant. Their parish-paid weekly income was forty-five dollars—not much money by today's standards, but more than ample for young newlyweds in 1943. Besides, forty-five dollars was more than double the *monthly* paycheck the army was handing out to most twenty-four-year-old young men, who did their praying in foxholes.

Billy made the best of his thirty-five parishioners, in the basement of a Western Springs meeting hall. With the help of Ruth and her missionary talent for numbers, he learned the ins and outs of the financial and business side of organized churchwork. The books balanced out, while Billy worked on his pulpit routine

66

until it sparkled and then caught the eye of a better-established Gospel spellbinder, the Reverend Torrey Johnson.

Johnson was well-known and well heeled in the big city of Chicago. He had founded the Midwest Bible Church, and by 1945 he had become the driving force behind the newest thing in evangelism, an organized soul-gathering road show called Youth for Christ.

But Torrey Johnson was more than just a prominent clergyman. He was a door opener. He knew all the right people in Chicago, and they, in turn, got to know his bright young protégé, Billy Graham. And just to make sure that everyone got to meet the newcomer, Johnson put Billy on Chicago radio once a week and gave him to the masses.

By 1945, Billy's reputation had outgrown Western Springs First Baptist. Rather than be held back by a small town any longer, he resigned from his pastorate and the radio show to work full-time for Torrey Johnson. Billy was picked to head the Youth for Christ crusade on its scheduled forty-seven-state sweep of the nation, in return for seventy-five dollars a week and a guarantee that he would learn tent-show evangelism from the bottom to the top. Spiritual and financial prospects were unlimited.

While Billy was on the road, getting his first taste of big crowds, Ruth headed home to Montreat on a crusade of her own, to find a small house to settle down in and await the arrival of little Virginia "Gigi" Graham, the first-born of the four Graham children. In the four years or so that followed, Ruth stayed close to home and to her parents. She watched from a domestic distance as Billy was vaulted to national prominence, with the help of the Hearst newspapers, and his resulting record-breaking, corner-turning Los Angeles revival of 1949. Ruth changed diapers while Billy changed into front-page big time.

1950 and Korea rolled around, and Billy reached a personal "Moment of Decision," leaving Torrey Johnson and Youth for Christ behind, to strike out on his own in the evangelical major leagues. Ruth stayed quietly on the sidelines, occasionally traveling with Billy but preferring to stay in Montreat, raising her growing brood and taking care of the household budget as best she could. In fact, Ruth's ability to scrimp and save became a legend around Montreat—and in the audit section of the Internal Revenue Service. The legend revolved around construction of a sprawling home for the Grahams.

There are several versions of the house-building story, none of which is entirely plausible, although most of them have been able to survive two and a half decades of skepticism and scrutiny.

The most popular account tells how Ruth cleaned out the sugar bowl in 1951 and purchased two hundred acres of prime Montreat hilltop woodland for a very sensible twenty-four hundred dollars. Another version makes the buy even more of a bargain, detailing how an unknown group of admiring North Carolina businessmen donated the land to Ruth and Billy as a token of esteem. (It's said that this same nameless benefactor still pays the property taxes.)

But it is common knowledge around Montreat that Ruth spent money at a six-figure annual rate in the 1950s, while Billy spent that decade crusading the world on his corporate allowance of fifteen to twenty thousand dollars a year.

Armed with unexplained cash, Ruth busied herself with drawings from expensive architects and made frequent forays into the surrounding farmlands, where she bought every old log cabin she could find, for fifty dollars apiece. Come building time, she said, the logs from these cabins would be used to give the new Graham home a simple, rustic look befitting the hilltop. To add another North Carolina backwoods touch, Ruth stockpiled antiques, which she bought from local residents for pennies, when they should have known better and demanded dollars.

While Ruth assembled the parts of the unconstructed home, she and Billy managed another budgetary miracle—they transformed a simple preacher's income into healthy trust funds, of unrevealed amounts, for each of the four children. Billy explained that the money came strictly from his book royalties and that all the complicated bookkeeping was handled by the people at his Minneapolis nonprofit corporation. After all, his business was saving souls, not high finance.

The building of the Graham dream house began in earnest in 1955 just as soon as Billy could rush home from his latest successful crusade to okay the final plans drawn up by Ruth's architect. Although it may be hard to visualize a hundred-thousand-dollar-plus pioneer barn raising, that's just the way it was described by Graham biographer Glenn Daniels.

> *Friends knew about Billy's attitude [against getting rich through the ministry]. They also knew that Ruth not only wanted, but needed a bigger house with more privacy.*
>
> *Several of them, therefore, volunteered to provide the labor and the material to build the house . . . provided they could remain anonymous in doing so, in order that Billy could not seek them out and prevent them from demonstrating their affection and gratitude.*

Stated in simpler terms, the Grahams get a very big and very expensive house, without having to pay, or account, for it.

These anonymous acts of charity worked like a charm. Not only did Billy *not* seek out the donors to say, "No, thank you," he and Ruth and the kids moved up onto the hill with a remarkable lack of protest for a family so outspoken against material gain.

Down below, and round about, a handful of doubters suggested (but never proved) that the Graham's "friends" were something more than just generous and affectionate. They were, claimed the nonbelievers, executives of Billy's own Twin Cities Evangelistic Association who had laundered tax-exempt corporate money for the boss.

It should be noted, without excessive comment, that the board that runs the Billy Graham Evangelistic Association, Incorporated, is heavily loaded with people who enjoy enviable life-styles thanks to Graham. Among them is Ruth, who may or may not draw a salary for not attending board meetings.

The story behind "The House That Ruth Built" is still a financial mystery to those outside the tightly closed Graham circle. But there is no mystery about why the home was built on an isolated hilltop and why it was designed like a fortress, with a commanding view toward every point of the compass.

Like his celebrated but fallen friend Richard Nixon, Billy Graham has become steadily obsessed by a fear of outsiders. He is reportedly in constant dread that someone will invade his off-stage privacy, whether with a harmless unannounced greeting or with a loaded revolver. And Billy's popularity has also brought with it uncounted death threats against him, Ruth, and the children.

Again like Richard Nixon, Billy has surrounded himself and his family with expensive domestic security rivaling that of the White House. The Graham hilltop is girdled by a double perimeter of electrified chain-link fence, with twenty-four-hour surveillance cameras, security patrols, and carefully screened bodyguards.

There is no special sign to mark the entrance to the Grahams' private winding road, which hairpins its way through monitored woods up to the house and its dead-bolt locks. There's merely a series of inhospitable signs reading, BEWARE VICIOUS DOGS. TRES-PASSERS WILL BE EATEN! Ruth put some of the signs there herself, years ago, even before the house was finished.

The warning is not to be taken lightly; the dogs are not to be confused with family pets. There are at least three large dogs who work behind the fences, all trained to respond to sixteen different attack commands in German. The dogs are trained to kill, if need be, although the need has not yet arisen.

Within these defenses, Ruth has grown to grand-motherhood, running the Graham household just as she has for thirty-four years. She still watches every penny in the "modest" household budget and makes sure that the maid and the handyman and the security people stay within the bounds of Billy's celebrated middle income. (It now stands at about twenty-five thousand dollars a year, to "keep up" with other, lesser-known clergymen.)

When the select few are invited to visit Ruth and Billy on the hilltop, they find something more than just a simple preacher's cottage. Technically speaking, it is a centrally air-conditioned, fully-convenienced ranch chalet, built to be new but look old. Nearly every room is provided with broad and varied picture-window views of the surrounding countryside below and the distant Smoky Mountains.

There is plenty of closet space to handle the lavish Graham wardrobes, linens, and other necessities "donated" by all those "friends" who always seem to be on hand when Ruth and Billy need something beyond their humble means.

It is a rich man's home, owned and operated by a man and a woman who insist they are not rich at all, just blessed by God and good connections.

These days, Billy still ventures forth from his fortress to go crusading, see to business, and play an occasional round of golf with the great and near great. And though the years are mounting against him, Billy Graham is still a full-time evangelist, and he's still the man at the top of a multimillion-dollar business-and-religious conglomerate.

But Ruth is, more than ever, the homebody, content to stay sheltered, protected, and out of sight within her opulent fortress. When she does pass through the gates of the guard fence, it's usually with Billy, and it's usually a short trip. In the old days, Ruth traveled on the long crusades and shared her husband's first-class accommodations, as well as his pulpit. Today, such Graham togetherness in public is a rare sight.

The secretive Graham life-style has long been a matter of image versus reality. Why must a man of God —and of the masses—hide himself behind warning signs and chain-link fences? Why has an undoubtedly clever, well-educated, talented woman played such a deliberately low-profile role in self-imposed isolation?

Is Ruth Graham just a simple preacher's housewife, or a clever manipulator of people and money who works best behind the scenes? Is she happy in her chosen life, or does she regret her decision to give up the challenge of missionary work, to become the wife of a well-known and well-off man?

The questions about Ruth and Billy are endless, but few answers are forthcoming, because the barriers have been built too high. What little the world knows about the Grahams and their relationship comes, not from observation, but through the suspect channels of the Billy Graham public-relations machine.

In her way, Ruth Graham fits into the American first-lady syndrome. Like Jacqueline, Lady Bird, Eleanor, and a string of others, Ruth is placed apart from other women because the man in her life is prominent and powerful. But unlike other first ladies, Billy Graham's wife has managed, by luck or careful design, to remain relatively free of public warts. The real Ruth Graham lives on a hilltop, safely out of reach.

Ruth has come a long way from Kiangsu province and a long way from that summer of 1941, when she found herself confronted by an unpleasant young truck driver on a small-town railroad-station platform. Whether the trip has been rewarding and fulfilling is known only to Ruth.

Lord knows, she looks happy enough with the way her life has worked out. But from this side of the electrified fence, the details are a bit too distant and blurred, and we really can't tell. Chances are, we'll never be invited inside the circle to ask Ruth who she really is and what she really feels. Billy and his guard dogs and Ruth just won't permit it.

4

Reblitzing Britain

*To disagree with three-fourths of
the British public on all points
is one of the first elements
of sanity.*

—OSCAR WILDE

If you really think about it, Jesus of Nazareth was one
hell of a good country Gospel preacher. He had it
all, and he could do it all. If you don't believe it, just
thumb through the New Testament, the official handbook on the Jesus technique.

The Prince of Peace was the evangelist's evangelist. He was humble, handsome, and helpful, not to mention merry, mild, and martyred. According to one popular account, he could even walk upon the waters.

William Franklin Graham did the same more than

nineteen hundred years later. Actually, the Reverend Billy Graham only walked on the waters in a highly technical, mortal sense, on the promenade deck of the Cunard Lines' *Queen Mary*, eastward-bound across the chilly North Atlantic, destined not to Galilee, but to Southampton, England.

Graham was floating, at twenty-two knots, to his first big crusade for souls in London. And although his savior might have objected to the first-class accommodations, the Reverend remained appropriately pious and publicly unspoiled.

Fellow passengers recall that he would stand alone for hours, gazing with determined evangelistic eyes toward the rolling horizon and the challenge ahead on the unseen shore. Graham held nightly Bible readings with his entourage and reportedly even spent time slumming in second and third class, saving several souls who weren't financially eligible to sit and break bread with the Lord at the first-class midnight buffets.

The Reverend Dr. Graham may have been at peace with his fellow passengers, and maybe even with the Lord, but the waiting British press was less pacific, causing publicity problems for the crusade even before the *Queen Mary* docked.

Crusty, professionally cynical journalists like Bill Connor of the *London Daily Mirror* got wind of Graham's fancy shipboard life-style and wondered about it in print. They pointed out that no true prophets went forth on luxury liners to do battle with the devil. Nor did they book themselves ahead in five-star hotels like the Kensington Palace, with its top-dollar (or pound, if you prefer) view of Hyde Park. Reverend Billy's hotel arrangements rivaled those of heads of state in England.

Graham flattened those observations with a practical swing of his well-worn Bible, backed up with homespun North Carolina common sense. "The Good Lord traveled on a donkey," he said. "If anybody can find me a donkey that can swim the Atlantic, I'll gladly oblige."

Experienced British writers suddenly realized that they were up against something more than just a former Fuller brush salesman, trying to get his foot in the Empire's door. In fact, he was already sitting in their living room, on their sofa, with his display case open and ready.

The London Crusade was going to be a spiritual, artistic, and financial success no matter what the writers and other detractors had to say about it. While British nonbelievers in Billy sat around calling him the Gabriel in Gabardine or the Bible-belt Barrymore, the smooth Graham advance men had been hard at work lining up every South Bank Protestant and every available London arena they could lay their hands on.

They had no need to worry about what it would all cost, because the Crusade team followed the financial wisdom set forth by England's William Shakespeare, who once wrote, "When in Rome, do as the Romans do." The Graham people just modified that to read, "When in London, let the Londoners foot the bill." The 1954 crusade was 95 percent locally funded or borrowed against long before Reverend Billy bought his passage in New York. The books were scrupulously British, with every single penny properly accounted for, to stand the test of even the most rigorous audits. Scores of Graham-hunters have spent whole careers going over the London crusade ledgers and have never found a shilling out of place. But that is only the paper story.

When Billy Graham looked down and smiled from the rail as the *Queen* moored at the Southampton quay, he had nothing to fear for his ultimate triumph. The stage had been carefully set, the scenario orchestrated. All he had to do was walk down the gangplank and do his thing.

Billy's spiritual ship had come in on schedule. Her Majesty's subjects were soon to experience a programmed panorama of pontification.

Over the years, the details of that London crusade have been dulled by time and retelling. But the highlights from the month or so Graham spent by the banks of the Thames simply can't be worn away. In a word, he knocked the English flat, whether they came forth for salvation or just remained in the back of the gallery with the devil.

During the days, he roared through a schedule that left the press, close aides, and well-wishers panting several lengths behind, inhaling the dust from his Florsheims. A spot of tea with the Queen at Buckingham Palace, a visit to the Tower of London, a trip to Parliament, a courtesy call on the Church of England, which hadn't rolled out the welcome mat yet, for dogmatic reasons. It was the same day in, day out, as Billy Graham reblitzed the ancient British capital.

But if Billy sparkled in the daylight, he was dazzling when the sun began to dip and the concert lights came on, to reveal the Greatest Salvation Show on Earth. Graham's crusade producers boast that their lighting is better than that at most rock concerts. One of their experts is a veteran of a Beatles tour.

There in the midst of his personal sea of white-robed Gospel singers, high on a platform for all to see and hear, was the thirty-seven-year-old legend in action.

That night in England, Graham was playing to a crowd that the North Carolina salesman could never have imagined in his wildest prepreaching days.

120,000 Britons had jammed their way into Wembley Stadium, converting what had been a dog-racing track into a temporary house of God, to the delight of the man on the podium, the concessionaires, and the religious record keepers. The throng at Wembley was the biggest ever recorded in the name of British Christianity or curiosity. The mark still stands. Only the Pope can claim a bigger turnout for one gathering—thanks in large part to a bigger place to pack the faithful in. But the holy father never had Graham's lighting or choreography.

Even the highest and the mightiest were impressed by the Miracle at Wembley. Lord Fisher, the Archbishop of Canterbury, gazed out over the multitude with misty eyes and remarked for Graham to hear, "We shall never see another sight like this until we are both in heaven." Unfortunately, England changes archbishops. And Billy was to fall from Grace.

Even Winston Churchill (of all people to be awe-stricken by mass adulation) cornered Graham after Wembley and candidly asked how the hell one man could draw such a huge crowd.

Billy came up with an appropriately modest explanation. "Winston," he said, "It's the power and support of God." Churchill chomped his Havana cigar and gave a noncommittal Churchillian grunt.

Giving credit to the Boss was, and still is, a Billy Graham crusader's trademark. But in 1954, Graham was doing plenty on his own to turn people out for the message the Boss wanted delivered. Overall, the first London crusade attracted more than 1.3 million through the turnstiles at big houses like Harringay Arena, home base of the running revival. And Lord knows how many others sat glued to television and radio sets, soaking up the word. Alas, the British rate of recidivism to sin is as high as the American during post-crusade periods.

Graham never seemed to lose public sight of his mission across the Atlantic, happily proclaiming that his open showman's style was saving souls and permanently changing lives. Many English clergymen still dispute this claim on both counts.

The Graham team kept careful count up front and reported that almost twenty-nine thousand people had been sufficiently impressed, or hell-fire frightened enough, to come forth and accept Jesus as their savior. That's an impressive number of converts even for Billy Graham, even though that cynical old British press corps had the audacity to suggest that most of the "newborn" would wind up back in sin. There seems to be a near hypnotic reaction by many who "come to the Lord" via Billy. They enjoy their salvation for a brief moment, then forget the whole thing.

The widely read British journalist Vincent Mulchrone went back in 1966 and checked relevant church records. He found that only about 30 percent of those who embraced Graham and God in 1954 were even bothering to show up in church twelve years later; that figure, clergymen said, would be no different if Graham hadn't left the *Queen Mary*.

But when Graham gathered up his steamer trunks and got back on the boat at the end of that first crusade, he wasn't thinking about the long-term dropout rate. For the time being, he could just sit back, relax, and enjoy another walk across the water, while his staff began working on plans for the crusades ahead. The early returns were good in Her Majesty's realm, and he could come back with booster talks for the backsliders.

The next dozen years saw Graham and his first-class-cabin following back in the United Kingdom no fewer than four full-dress times. Each time he found the press energetically nitpicking him in print and more organized churches in England, Scotland, Ireland, and Wales increasingly less impressed with his visits. The new archbishop of Canterbury (not so easily impressed as the old one at Wembley) publicly attacked Billy Graham for showboating. Clergymen, the archbishop said, "shouldn't wave Bibles or sweat while doing God's will."

The comment was a low blow, to be sure, because Graham had always perspired more than most for the Lord. Under the properly filtered red, blue, green, and yellow lights (and he always uses properly filtered hot lights), Graham had dropped thirty-two pounds in 1954. His wife, Ruth, still takes pride in recounting how her husband mastered the old stage art of the quick change, ducking out of sight during a musical interlude or hat-passing session to replace his sweat-soaked clothes, right down to underwear and socks. It kept him natty and crisp no matter how hot and heavy the sermon, but it gave fire to the traditionalists in England as they scorched Graham's crusades.

The archbishop of Canterbury's criticism of Reverend Billy's sweat glands was more than it seemed on the surface. It was an unusual outburst of theological bad mouth flung by church leaders at Graham between 1954 and 1964. He had become a symbol of the Anglican failure to keep, much less boost, the size of its congregation. Graham was packing them in every time he popped up in London, Glasgow, Manchester, or anywhere else he picked to preach.

He was making the organized church look stuffy and backward. And rather than admit they were stuffy and backward, clerics like the archbishop did the next best thing. They huffed, puffed, and denounced Billy

Graham as just another troublesome radical trying to upset the spiritual applecart. But whatever the motives of the Church of England's hierarchy, Billy's "Allstar" approach and slick theatrics helped sour a large segment of the British population.

On the other side of the pulpit, the truly radical religious leaders of Great Britain looked upon Billy Graham as too conservative. Unlike their elders, they feared he wasn't tipping the cart, but pulling it along the path.

Of course, while his British colleagues quibbled over who was really right, Graham went straight ahead and crusaded, bigger and better than ever (with more lights and choir members than ever). There were more Wembleys and Harringays and multi-city television simulcasts. Crusade budgets soared to the half-million-dollar mark, but the revenue matched the budgets, and the books kept right on balancing.

By March 1964, the Billy Graham road-show momentum had gathered so much popular steam in Britain that another super crusade seemed very much in order. Forsaking a ship ride in favor of speed, Graham jetted to London, armed with the blueprint for the biggest revival ever staged.

On March 19, he stood before twenty-five hundred churchmen who hadn't yet turned their backs on him, and he ticked off the details of what was to come. In just two years, he said, he'd launch the greatest gathering of souls in the history of the British Empire. 1966 was to be the big year for the converted English Christian.

When asked why he'd decided to go all out in London again, despite the press, defectors, and the archbishop, Graham gave an answer any modern-day Englishman could understand. It was all because of

John Lennon, Paul McCartney, Ringo Starr, and George Harrison, a quartet of successful agnostics called the Beatles.

As Graham explained it, "I never watch television on Sunday, but the temptation to watch the Beatles [on Ed Sullivan's Show] was a little too great, so I tuned in. All I heard was the screaming of three thousand young people. I do not know what they were feeling, but I think that in the church we have gone too far not being emotional. We need to have some feeling in our faith!"

It's no surprise that mixing theological strategy with top-forty frenzy didn't sit well with the old archbishop and the rest of England's traditional church leaders. But then, it wasn't intended to. Billy Graham was playing casually to the galleries again and getting valuable space and time in the media. On March 20, 1964, the *Daily Mail* recounted the Beatle speech, under a headline that proclaimed with glee, THE TEMPTATION OF BILLY GRAHAM! And a nameless feature writer for the venerable *London Times* may have overreacted when he praised Graham for "feeling the shortcomings of the Church and the rock-beat Pulse of the Nation." Was Graham actually going to offer God through stereo speakers, or was it just a gesture to attract the young?

The spark of curiosity had been struck again. Billy Graham waved goodbye to well-wishers at Heathrow Airport and stepped aboard his homebound flight, leaving behind his aura of goodness—and leaving behind his team of advance men and local contacts who would spend the next two years busily making sure everything would be just right for a British preview of Woodstock with angels.

In 1966, London was going to be saved as it had never been saved before, whether they liked it or not.

The morning of May 24, 1966, dawned gray and damp and routine for Southampton. Over at the Cunard Lines docking area, stevedore crews and baggagemen began drifting in from the streetside, through the dark cavern of the customs shed, toward the carts and loading machinery lined along the quay. The smell of the oily water drifted up from the pilings and mixed with the exhaust from an idling tugboat, waiting to take a chest of ice aboard for the long day's work ahead.

A railroad traffic man zigzagged across the shed area, searching in vain for someone from Cunard to complain to. People were lining up along the tracks with WELCOME BILLY GRAHAM banners, and the trainman wanted them moved out of the way before someone got hurt. But oblivious to the potential dangers, the devout members of the growing throng just milled about. Some practiced their hymns. (To make certain the group was enthusiastic enough, twenty professionals were hired. The rest really were volunteers.)

Fifteen miles away, the engine-room telegraph clanged to Dead Slow and then to Full Stop/All Engines as the *Queen Mary* began a long coasting maneuver to come into line with three large sea-going tugs. The weather was clearing now, and thin sunshine warmed the passengers who were already jockeying for good vantage points on the landward rails of the decks.

Dining stewards wrestled with trays of last-call breakfast dishes belowdecks, and cabin stewards piled luggage by the large off-loading hatches, taking care to pyramid each heap of Samsonite so nothing would topple in case the *Queen* should make a sudden lurch.

Billy and Ruth Graham had been up since the first light. First of all, to pray, just as "they always did together on land or sea." They had an early breakfast with other members of the crusade entourage, then

84

went their separate ways—Ruth, to attend to the last-minute packing and the tip for the steward; Billy, to go over the list of fifty questions he had jotted down during the crossing.

Experience had taught Billy Graham that reporters were not the bottomless pits of curiosity they thought themselves to be. In more than twenty-five years of news conferences, he had categorized the questions aimed at him, time and again, and narrowed them to just half a hundred. During this trip he had decided to update the list a bit, to be prepared for new, more eager reporters who might want to stump him about the escalating American involvement in the Vietnam war. He did not want to be caught off-guard and accidentally take sides in the issue.

Back on land, the previous calm at the docks had been replaced by beehive activity at the first glimpse of the lumbering *Queen* on the horizon. Overalled men jostled through officials and welcoming parties of all sizes and descriptions. And out on the street, by the rail siding, someone gave a false alarm. The Graham crusaders (now about sixty of them) began cheering and singing by mistake.

Customs officials were already at their places, going over the passenger lists and manifests brought in by a Cunard representative on the returning pilot boat. Pens flicked over checklists and rubber stamps thumped in triplicate, while word went round customs that Graham and his party were not to be detained, but sent straightaway to a pair of reserved rail coaches. That special treatment was reserved for entertainers and politicians—and superstar evangelists, who might be described as being a little bit of both.

By ten in the morning, the *Queen* loomed high above the dockside, drifting sideways the last few feet

85

into her restraining gear. Passenger doors and cargo hatches were already open, and covered gangways swung into proper position.

Onboard, a docker was busily coiling a rope on the promenade deck, when he looked up and came face to face with the passenger he'd heard about the entire trip but had never seen. "That's Bill the Bible Puncher!" he hollered in his best salt.

Graham either did not hear the remark or chose to ignore it, but the docker persisted and gave it one more shot. He dropped his coil and pointed to the mass of people six decks below and proclaimed, "Look! There's a load out there that wants savin'!" This time, the preacher wheeled around, cracked his best-polished evangelist smile, and gave the seaman the good, old-fashioned high sign, thumbs up.

Bill the Bible Puncher had met his first challenge of the new crusade with style and grace. The docker even tipped his hat in honor of the victory at his expense. Great Britain had better be ready for the sixties' version of mellifluous salvation.

Graham and his wife disembarked from the *Queen* shortly before 11:00 A.M. and were met by a waiting delegation of clergymen, civic leaders, journalists, and hangers-on. One writer in the crush recalls that Graham looked almost the same as he had twelve years before, except he was a little heavier around the waist and, perhaps, a little bit thinner and grayer on top.

Another British reporter, who had been aboard during the whole passage, noted that he watched from the gangway as Graham and his wife were swallowed up by the engulfing crowd. He feared the couple would be hurt in the confusion.

Through it all, Billy Graham smiled and clutched his well-worn black-leather-bound Bible. When people tear at his clothes or pass him gifts, he turns them aside with the skill of a presidential campaigner, murmuring, "Bless you, bless you," over and over again. Meanwhile, Graham's aides use sophisticated crowd-control techniques with the confidence of the Secret Service.

Outside the customs area, the Graham party paused, not because it wanted to, but because the private coaches were not yet ready for boarding. Graham looked disturbed by the wait but continued his *bless yous*, fixed smile, waves and handshakes.

Hymns and chants of "Billy, Billy, Billy" mixed in the air, prompting a man from the *Daily Mail* to report the next day, "The crowd was struck slightly dumb by his presence, like so many Indian peasants content with the 'darshan' blessing which comes with being in mere contact with the great."

The *Daily Mail* article went on to note that Graham hadn't lost his sense of timing or his knack for saying the right thing at the right time, even while waiting on a platform for a train.

According to the account, the whistle blew, the conductor yelled, " 'Board!" and Graham turned to the crowd and proclaimed, "This time, we'll focus our eyes on the Lord and *not* on me!"

The boat-train rolled away from the platform toward London's Waterloo Station at exactly 11:16 in the morning. At the same time there was speculation that Billy Graham had made it clear he was going to behave himself this crusade and play the game the way the English churchmen wanted him to. Packed in all those steamer trunks, rumor had it, was an olive branch.

But it turned out that the olive branch was wrapped around a righteous club that Graham began swinging the very next day, in the gilded surroundings of the main banquet room in London's Waldorf Hotel.

Billy Graham strode into the room to face reporters with a finger-waving and podium-pounding denunciation of the lack of British morality.

He stood there and told Greater London that it stood on the very brink of hell, with one leg already burned off up to the knee. And he issued a warning that he, for one, wasn't going to let the devil move into 10 Downing Street.

"London is the moral capital of the world," he cried. "But it's on the road to decadence. I intend to preach the Gospel as the solution to man's problems. I wish I could take people and shake them and say, 'This is the answer!' "

The performance rattled the Waldorf's chandeliers and inspired the *Evening Standard*'s Jonathon Aitken to rush back to his city room to bat out a two-column warning to England that the same old Billy Graham was back again.

> *The first fierce shots of Billy Graham's Greater London Crusade were fired today at the Waldorf.*
>
> *Almost every question produced an uninspiring sermon out of forty-seven-year-old Graham whose seventy-five-minute performance showed that, besides being a successful evangelist, he would clearly be an equally successful politician, diplomat, juggler or show business impressario.*

Aitken had a front-row seat for the Waldorf performance, and he continued his article with a blow-by-blow description of the master in action. His description of Supersaver that day is a classic:

> *In moments of stress, Dr. Graham gripped his Bible like a squash racquet. So vehemently, in fact, that at one point he knocked over his waterglass.*
>
> *The most mesmeric things about Billy*

88

> *Graham were his gestures. Mick Jagger is a statue*
> *by comparison. The hand on the heart . . . the*
> *menacingly wagging finger . . . the chop . . . the*
> *clenched fists . . . the fluttering wrists.*
>
> *When making moral judgments, he stretches*
> *out both hands and gazes heavenward, like a crick-*
> *et-player trying to catch a skier [fly ball].*
>
> *To emphasize a point, he whips two pointing*
> *fingers from behind his back at six-gun drawing*
> *speed.*
>
> *When the Word of God is about to come*
> *forth, he puts his hand to his mouth, as though he*
> *is plucking out a piece of imaginary chewing gum*
> *. . . which he then proceeds to stick on the micro-*
> *phone.*

Aitken concluded his first-hand observations of the news conference with the flat statement that Graham hadn't done any better at Wembley in 1954. He added, "No one could have missed the message. The 1966 Greater London Crusade was going to top anything that had come before. There's no business like save business."

This time, the Crusade was going to cost someone other than the Billy Graham crusade organization upwards of three hundred thousand pounds, or $800,000. And, instead of calling Harringay Arena home, it would open on June 1 in the exhibition hall at Earl's Court, a place big enough to hold the twenty-seven thousand lost souls expected nightly.

Graham's team, applying lessons learned in crusades in the States, had set up a radio and television network that covered every corner of the British Isles. The message was being wired into every home for every potential convert.

Just to make sure that every base was covered, the

crusade's organizers had enlisted an army of freshly scrubbed, devoted young volunteers to invade every possible sin-ridden street corner, pub, and strip joint. So many leaflets were printed for the onslaught that there were jokes that England might sink into the sea under their weight. The youth look was something Graham cultivated carefully at the time of the Beatles and Vietnam.

All of this prompted Vincent Mulchrone to break out his typewriter to try to put things into his own doubting perspective. On May 25, 1966, he wrote:

> The smoothest evangelistic machine of modern times has preceded Graham to London . . . to be received, yet again, by the Church of England with less than open arms.
>
> But Billy Graham is not dismayed. "This time will be different from 1954," he told me. "Today we are nearer the end of our spiritual ropes."

Mulchrone was a veteran Graham watcher. He'd followed every crusade with an eye for the nuance and detail. And he told his readers that this biggest of all crusades might not come off very well:

> In 1954, Graham was a crusader. But familiarity has made him something cosier. After twelve years and four crusades, we've grown accustomed to his faith.
>
> The one thing his otherwise "with it" team has overlooked is the infinite British capacity for absorbing disturbing phenomena, whether in people or in movements, and smothering them with polite understanding.
>
> If Billy Graham stayed here six months, rather than one, the result would be spiritual boredom

90

> *. . . not for us, but for him. It is our spiritual in-*
> *difference that will depress him, not our opposition.*

Mulchrone summed his gloomy predictions up in one neat analogy:

> *We'll buy Billy Graham this time around like we*
> *buy the* War Cry *in a pub . . . not to offend but*
> *not to join either.*

The cynical press notwithstanding, Billy Graham pressed forward with his plans, using the days between his Southampton landing and the big opening to best possible advantage—that is, getting his picture and his ideas into print and onto the air.

Quotable quotes abounded from his lips on topics ranging from the threat of world annihilation to hair styles and music. He said plenty about "blatant sex" and about his conclusion that Merrie England was in the grips of a nonstop orgy that would destroy the nation.

"Great Britain has an obsession with sex," he told a May 26 gathering of reporters. "To read the papers and the magazines here, you would think we were almost worshiping the female bosom."

Graham put the big-chest fixation in terms befitting the pulpit. "When people lose their way, their purpose, their will, and their goals, as well as their faith—like the ancient Israelites, they go awhoring."

It should be noted that in the period since that warning the number of prostitutes in London has increased five-fold, according to a *London Times* survey.

On the heated subject of miniskirts, Graham told newsmen he neither approved or disapproved. Diplomatically, he left the final decision on fashions to Ruth, who only smiled in her below-the-knee skirt.

As always, Graham set the keynote of his upcoming crusade with a standard evangelist's trick—the threat of Armageddon, just around the corner. People don't surrender their souls to a higher authority unless they are worried enough to hand over the reins. The material was old, but it still seemed to do the trick.

The spectre Graham raised was familiar. He'd been using it since the dawn of the atomic age and the settling in of the cold war. "Only a fool will believe today that we are not heading for a worldwide showdown, when nuclear power is spreading to so many nations. The world is heading for the judgment, and if we think we can solve our problems without God, we are wrong."

It was the same page out of the basic script from "The Hour of Decision," Graham's radio program. In fact, Mordecai Ham had probably used the same basic line when teenaged Billy Graham was standing in the back of the tent, unconverted. The only real difference was the degree of the judgment at hand. Ham didn't have nuclear weapons to wave over the heads of the crowds.

On the eve of the June 1 Earl's Court opening, much of the United Kingdom clustered around television sets to watch Graham "just be himself" on a BBC talk show called "About Religion." Normally, the audience for the program was sparse and sleepy. But on May 31, it drew an audience like "Upstairs, Downstairs."

Graham was a picture of corduroy-sports-jacket comfort, all neatly combed and fully prepared to bare *his* soul to the people on the other side of the red lights.

He kept in such marvelous shape, he told his interviewers, with a rigid daily program of physical fitness. A two-mile jog every day, rain or shine, followed by a half hour of other exercises. Add plenty of sleep and green salads and prayer, and God's work could be done, without the threat of wear and tear or loss of that famous flat-hipped Billy Graham physique.

Turning from keeping in shape to getting society back into shape, Graham warned the British nation to pay attention to its children and what they were trying to say. He said the kids were being strange and obnoxious and emulating the Beatles and the Rolling Stones because they were in search of life's true meanings.

"The exhibitionism of many young people is part of a spiritual search." So was the use of drugs, he added, and wild, unbridled sex and disrespect for elders and institutions. In fact, the youth of Great Britain was searching so much for the truth that it threatened to bring the Empire down in an instant replay of Sodom and Gomorrah.

Graham was ready for the next hard question fired his way, because it had been on his top-fifty list since the early 1950s, and he knew the response by heart, just like his favorite Bible passages.

"About Religion" host Kenneth Harris wanted to know whether Jesus Christ would approve of preachers' buying time on television to spread the gospel.

Graham leaned forward, cocked an eyebrow, at the camera and let fly, "If Jesus were alive today, I believe he would use television, because he used every means at his disposal.

"I can preach to more people in one night on TV than, perhaps, Paul did in his whole lifetime, simply because I now have a means of communicating the Gospel to more people."

With that, Billy Graham gathered up his media advisors and makeup man and limousined back to his suite at the Waldorf to pray, take thirty minutes of exercise and fall asleep, perhaps to dream of his next day's conquest at Earl's Court.

One Billy Graham performance was pretty much like all the others during that month of June 1966. Packed galleries fanned themselves with the programs, while Billy's warm-up men got the ball rolling with the standard welcomes and the crusade chorus fleshed out the proceedings with hum-alongs. There were a few new lighting effects, amazingly similar to production gimmicks on recent American network musical specials.

Then the big hush, followed by the teary-eyed ovation as the Man and his Suit swept into the hall, up the stairs, and across the platform to the floodlit pulpit.

With palms raised for silence, William Franklin Graham began each sermon with the same light-handed touch of a Kiwanis after-dinner toastmaster. He began with plenty of parables and anecdotes to get the crowd nicely quiet and paying attention for the serious thumping, bumping, and warnings.

By the time Billy got to the scripture part about nuclear showdowns and second comings, people would invariably jump the gun and start wandering down to the front of the hall to be saved, off-cue. But the rest of the house generally waited for Graham to proclaim the "moment of decision" before joining the eager few who had bumbled ahead into the orchestra pit and found, not God, but the piano player, drinking a Coke.

It was the same show every night, until the scheduled run was over and the final head counting began. According to Graham aides, some forty thousand Londoners had taken the walk and made their personal decisions for Christ. Figured against the cost of the crusade, it worked out to an expenditure of about five

pounds (thirteen dollars) per soul, a hefty hike in per-
capita salvation, thanks to rampant British inflation and
the high cost of broadcast time.

But Graham was generous, in a spiritual sort of
way, about the incredible expense. "If the crusade had
won just one convert," he observed, "then I would have
considered it a success."

With the record-breaking London crusade completed, the Graham organization packed up like a circus
and moved to other English cities that had money to
spend in the name of Christ. The summer dragged on
toward fall while the Church of England looked on with
increasing and predictable disquiet.

By October 1966 the Archbishop of Canterbury
was back at it, casting large stones at Billy Graham in
the press. Dr. Ramsey still found it tacky for Graham to
go about the land getting emotionally involved with his
God. The archbishop much preferred a less disturbing,
more intellectual approach to bringing in the sheaves.

For his trouble, Ramsey found himself the target of
public criticism, such as an article in the *Sun*, written on
October 4, by Richard Last.

The headline over the story read, COME OFF IT
ARCHBISHOP! and the article warned the head of the
church that he might wind up splitting his forces over
Billy Graham. Last wrote, "There is no doubt that a
large portion of the Anglican clergy . . . possibly more
than half . . . are firmly on Billy Graham's side this time
around.

"A number are claiming additions to their congregations as a direct result of Billy Graham's preaching."

The Last article, and others like it, never spelled
out which clergymen, or exactly how many, had rallied
to Graham's side. And no one could detail just how
many converts suddenly began occupying pews each

Sunday or how long they kept their newfound habit of regular attendance.

This was just like all the other times Billy Graham had worked the British circuit. His crusaders declared victory for the Lord, and his critics denied it. Thousands had come forth, then gone off somewhere to either stay with God or slowly forget about him. Only one thing could be said with assurance, by either side—evangelizing was not like studying the migration of birds. You couldn't put tags on converts to see if they flew back to church each Sunday.

Measured in sheer attendance figures and friendly popular response, the 1966 London crusade had more or less lived up to its two-year billing. It had been the biggest and best one to date. Before passing back through Southampton, Graham announced he would be back to the hub of the Empire to keep his hand in and make sure the devil stayed his distance from Christian Englishmen.

The last of the full-fledged Billy Graham crusades on British soil came in August and early September 1973. Of the lot, it was the most controversial and certainly the least successful in terms of broad appeal and total souls "saved."

For one thing, Graham's political timing was not the best when he flew into Heathrow on the evening of August 23. In the seven years since the Earl's Court campaign, some of Billy's carefully rehearsed neutrality had worn away. He'd finally come out in semisupport of the United States' role in Vietnam. Just as bad, Graham had warmly embraced Richard M. Nixon as his friend and golfing buddy. Now both Nixon and the Vietnam war were on the skids in British public esteem, and Graham slipped a bit with them. Graham's comments and Nixon's mutterings sometimes seemed interchangeable.

For another thing, Graham had changed his entrance style and approach since the glory, hallelujah! days of 1966. This time he arrived without parade, fanfare, or the adoring crowds of the past. So modest was his unheralded landing, that only a handful of staffers were at hand to meet him at the airport. Most of Greater London and most of the Graham team hadn't even been warned he was coming in that night. This arrival bore none of the glitter and triumph of a *Queen Mary* arrival—perhaps because the *Queen Mary* was sitting in Long Beach, California, converted to a tourist attraction and floating snack bar; perhaps because Billy Graham had been converted to a different kind of evangelist. Something or someone was out of phase.

Even the basic approach was different this time. The crusade was to be called Spree 73, which sounded more like a late-summer back-to-school Macy's sale than a Southern Baptist revival. Actually, *Spree* stood for "Spiritual Re-Emphasis." The planners had laid it out, not as a crusade, but as a "youth-oriented happening." This time, Graham told reporters, he was in London primarily to help young followers of Christ get together and share the faith they already possessed. Somehow, that idea seemed lazy and out of character when measured against the past.

In the old days, Billy had swept into London surrounded by his white-robed multitudes and the other time-tested trappings of big-production evangelism. So it was a considerable shock to many, when he unveiled the cast of Spree 73, especially the new backup men who would share the dais.

Among them was a former bad-boy 1950s rock star

named Terry Dene, who had given up years of brooding about his lost fame to become an evangelist. Along with Dene was America's best-known monotonic former prison inmate, singer Johnny Cash—a genuine Billy Graham convert.

Spree 73 was not to be a long-drawn-out affair like most past crusades. It was booked for a one-week stand in the ever-popular Wembley Stadium and at Earl's Court. But the total cost was placed at more than three hundred and fifty thousand pounds, an all-time high. Critics called the sum a bit extravagant, in light of Great Britain's running battle against national bankruptcy.

But Billy Graham was not particularly concerned with the state of the exchequer or the problems of a middle-class family. His almost undivided attention was aimed at the personal task at hand—to consolidate his influence on the hearts and souls of young Britons who wanted to follow the Christian teachings set forth so well in the lyrics and lighting effects of *Jesus Christ, Superstar*: the Gospel According to Broadway. And if it took a few upbeat hymns by Johnny Cash and some extra bucks, so be it.

On September 2, 1973, the new approach clicked at Wembley Stadium, although the turnout fell about ninety thousand short of the miracle mark of 1954. London read about it the next morning in the pages of the *Mirror*:

> *Wembley Stadium's big tote-board tells people the name of the first and second in the correct finishing order. But it wasn't the dogs finishing at Wembley yesterday.*
> *More than thirty thousand youngsters demon-*

> *strated they were putting Jesus Christ first, with*
> *Billy Graham and Johnny Cash a close second.*
>   *Tieless, and wearing a brown corduroy jacket,*
> *Billy Graham delivered a rollicking Sermon on the*
> *Turf.*
>   *The new converts sang, swayed, clapped*
> *hands and smiled with evangelical enthusiasm.*
> *And, through it all, Billy Graham sat on the stage,*
> *clapping and smiling along with them, while an*
> *expensive battery of equipment recorded the rally*
> *for his own film company.*

No self-respecting multimedia master would miss a chance like that. Graham's advisors had correctly told him that a young audience is far more animated when the cameras point toward them.

While the young people cavorted for the cameras, attractive Spree girls passed, like cheerleaders, among the faithful with collection buckets in one hand and Billy Graham crusade LPs in the other. Johnny Cash Gospel eight-tracks did a good turnover, and Spree 73 T-shirts sold out in small, medium, and large. The money rolled in, and the rallies rolled on to a rock-a-Billy conclusion. And Billy Graham proved that he could still draw a crowd in London, even if he had to do it with a rock concert instead of the simple promise of everlasting life.

That's not to say that Spree 73 was a road-company Woodstock. There were no naked people jumping in the pond, and clouds of marijuana smoke never materialized to hang in midair like a holy ghost. Looking back on it all, the proceedings were not as far out as they seemed at the time. A week after it was all over, the *Daily Telegraph* reflected on the big event, "Graham provided an entertainment tailor-made for the audience of apprentice missionaries . . . pop music with the decadence *vacuumed out.*"

The Billy Graham presence is still very much alive in London and the rest of the United Kingdom, just as it is in the United States and most of the Bible-reading world. His name is a household word, and he is a repeated visitor to England's shores. And although his return trips are more solo than multitudinous, he still sparks those same old feelings of love and hate that first rose up in British breasts twenty-three years ago.

There is really no way to gauge what true spiritual effect, if any, he has worked on the English. He probably couldn't tell you that himself. Overall, Billy Graham's impact on the British has been more clearly emotional than anything else. Everyone, it seems, has a feeling about the man, even if his message leaves them colder than a leftover Yorkshire pudding.

It has already been noted that Billy Graham's friendship with the fallen Richard Nixon has dismayed and disappointed many Britons who expected him to keep better, more honest company. Graham's running defense of the former president may, indeed, be a personal act of Christian charity—but it has not appeared that way across the Atlantic. Instead of appearing kind-hearted, Graham has taken on the aura of a Nixonian crony.

Daily Mirror writer John Pilger suggests that change of image underlines Billy Graham's basic weakness all these years: superficiality, neatly hidden by evangelistic sleight of hand:

> *Billy Graham's power and influence, and that of his multi-million-dollar corporation in Milwaukee (sic), has been a fact since the 1950's.*

100

> *But, during all these years it has never been*
> *clear what . . . apart from God . . . he believes in.*
> *And what . . . apart from Jesus Christ . . . he is*
> *committed to.*

That assessment is not unique to the *Mirror*. It now confronts him in every city and country where he appears. It confronts him but does not prompt him to explain where he really stands when he leaves the pulpit.

These days Billy Graham is treated like a long-standing celebrity in the British media. His name pops up in the columns along with those of Sammy Davis, Muhammad Ali, and Richard Burton. He is often quoted in print, but the topics of discussion are usually less than almighty in their weight and importance.

For example, on March 6, 1974, Graham waved aside all questions about his role in the romance of British television personality David Frost. Hollywood gossip columnist Joyce Haber said she had it on good authority that Frost and leggy fashion model Karen Graham planned to marry on the QT, with Billy Graham tying the knot.

Billy had no comment on the story. Frost was livid, protesting he'd wanted the ceremony to be quiet and simple, free from flashbulbs and fanfare. Ms. Graham said nothing and quietly ditched Frost at the altar, to run off and marry an automobile salesman.

In 1975, Billy Graham was back in the London papers, although the articles occupied space on the back pages, not up front where the banners had used to fly. He was widely quoted as saying UFOs might really be God's angels in disguise. That at least is an improvement over an earlier Graham pronouncement that New York policemen were angels in blue.

101

The fire and frenzy of the Billy Graham crusades are gone now from the United Kingdom. Only the embers remain, to be occasionally fanned a little brighter by his nostalgic side trips. Whether there will be yet another massive transatlantic campaign rests in the back of his mind, unmentioned, unplanned, and unimportant to England. In reality, it's doubtful that Graham will ever stand in the midst of another Wembley record-breaker. He's on the threshold of age sixty and occupied with his nonstop missions in the United States. To pull off 1954 and 1966 again might be just too much for one mortal preacherman to do, even with the help of God, his heavenly hosts, and the best lighting and promotion people in the business.

In spite of all the triumphs and souls that Billy Graham collected in Great Britain over the years, that island nation remains just about as sin-sick and wayward as when Graham's gangplank first rolled out almost a quarter century ago. Chances are it will stay that way until Billy Graham's boss decides to launch his second and final crusade . . . and returns to earth for the long-awaited count on who really came forth and meant it.

The Graham team isn't worried about the final judgment. After all, the books have always balanced, and, God willing, they always will.

5

The Magic-carpet
Messiah

I look upon the world as my parish.
　　　　　　—JOHN WESLEY

Anybody who feels at ease in the
world today is a fool!
　　　　　—ROBERT MAYNARD HUTCHINS

There's more to overseas crusading than just looking out for the needs of the tiny United Kingdom. What
Billy Graham and his Gospel gypsies began twenty-
three years ago in London has since spread around the
globe to every major continent and island group in the
atlas. Only the penguins, white bears, and Eskimos of
the polar regions have escaped Billy's personal visits—
although his radio programs can be picked up on short
wave in the Arctic and Antarctic wastes.

Since 1954, Billy has traveled through almost seventy-five countries and hundreds of cities, towns, and hamlets within their distant borders. East, west, north, and south, he's pounded the Bible everywhere, even under the watchful eye of Soviet tanks in divided Berlin and from the back of a half track in the Egyptian desert. Tape recordings of his best sermons have even been translated, on the spot in the jungles of New Guinea.

If his alleged overseas converts were placed end to end they would stretch from Timbuktu to the doorstep of the United Nations building. At least, that's the way the Graham publicity mill likes to estimate the figures.

Billy wears his international crusades like jewels in his self-donned preacher's crown. They glitter and show the world that his magic and message appeal to all men, in all places. But in truth, Billy's overseas revivals aren't one bit different in basic format, execution, or outcome from the ones we have come to know by heart right here on the home turf. In Paris, Oslo, or even Jerusalem, it's the same old routine—a little bit of oversimplified Gospel, a touch of hell fire, a pitch for local currency, a Moment of Decision, and a generous helping of spotlight theatrics. The only difference between a rally in Milwaukee and one in Dortmund, Germany, is the language—and the local brew.

And since a rose is a rose and a crusade is a crusade, there isn't much need to provoke eyestrain in these pages with a litany of who Billy preached to, where, why, and for how long. (If you're really interested in all that, just check the index.) We'll discuss, instead, a few of Billy's most fabulous foreign forays and try to see why they weren't always the miracles his press brochures claimed them to be.

The Star of India

On the snow-flecked morning of January 15, 1956, Billy Graham grinned his way out of New York's Statler Hotel with a brown calfskin-covered Bible in one hand and a book of Hindu philosophy in the other. At the carefully orchestrated urging of everyone except the Roman Catholic Church, he was on his way to India for a one-month evangelistic shot against long odds in one of the world's most overpopulated, under-Christianized nations.

A number of his own followers doubted that an Indian crusade could be pulled off. Preaching the Gospel in Bombay is like walking into a kosher delicatessen and ordering a ham sandwich on white with mayonnaise.

But that's the very reason Billy and his closest aides accepted the invitation and the challenge of the Evangelical Fellowship of India. As the well-publicized underdog, Billy could reap a whirlwind of media coverage, whether his mission to India succeeded or not.

There were political benefits to be gained as well. With the blessings of President Eisenhower and Secretary of State John Foster Dulles, Billy headed toward India deliberately to upstage Soviet Premier Nikita Khrushchev. Indian Prime Minister Nehru and his teeming masses had given the ham-fisted Russian a much-too-warm welcome in 1956 and it was clearly up to Billy to balance the scales for the benefit of America's Asian allies and enemies. As far as the State Department image makers were concerned, the Graham crusade provided the much-needed second act of a morality play.

To make sure there was an audience when the curtain went up, the Graham advance men pulled out all

the stops with every Broadway promotion technique at
their skilled command. Weeks before Billy checked out
of the Statler, India was bombarded with crusade
advertising—everything from broadcast trucks to broad-
sheets nailed to local trees. There had never been a
campaign like it in India. The masses were bewildered
but curious—and that was the whole Madison
Avenue–inspired idea. Make 'em curious enough to
come out and watch.

   With the help of Dulles and his minions, Billy was
hooked in to Nehru and every other Westernized Brahmin along the crusade route. The Evangelical Fellowship was put under nonstop pressure to line up every
Christian who could be tracked, trained, and trotted out
to throw flowers at the feet of the Great Visitor. According to some very ill-kept records, there are ten million
Christians in India—not many in a nation of more than
four hundred million, unless they could all be brought
together at one time, in one place, for the distorting eye
of the camera.

   To maximize the chances of getting a decent turn-
out, Billy was booked into cities with established
Christian communities—Bombay, Delhi, Kottayam, and
Madras—with a few side stops like Calcutta thrown in.
But despite careful planning, the itinerary derailed at
the very top of the list, when Billy touched down in
Bombay.

   The city was abusing itself with another round of
language riots, and Billy's security people were reluctantly forced to cancel the first big outdoor rallies,
rather than risk an ad lib uprising in midsermon. To
recoup his embarrassing loss, Billy rented a safe indoor
hall for a series of sweat-soaked meetings with friendly
ministers and missionaries. To spread the word a bit
further, he launched a series of news conferences with

leading Indian newspaper and magazine men. Overall he found them intellectual and hostile, critical of his methods and outspokenly suspicious of his motives.

Leading the pack was a troublesome Western-educated journalist named P. Lal, editor of Calcutta's well-read and well-respected *Orient Review*. Lal was not impressed by the world's most sensational evangelist, and he said so in print:

"According to Indian tradition, the religious man is marked by humility, charity and a degree of asceticism; his 'worldliness' is supposed to be displayed in performing social services in the villages of the hinterland.

"Immaculate blue suits, a wife and children, spotlights and microphones are not regarded as a suitable 'environment' for a religious leader."

Lal and a disturbing number of his Indian colleagues were offended by the way Billy talked down to them during the conferences. The editor of the Bombay *Illustrated Weekly* complained that the preacher's "way of parrying reporters' questions with Bible quotations made it seem as if he was delivering a pulpit address."

Lal accused Billy of putting on airs in an effort to sell the crusade image to the Indian press corps. "It is paradoxical that Dr. Graham . . . who succeeds in turning his sermons into a kind of chatty, personal talk . . . tends to transform his press conferences . . . which should be chatty and personal . . . into sermons."

Instead of listening to what Lal and the others were saying, Billy and his advisers stuck to their game plan: to impose a Western-culture crusade on a country that neither wanted nor understood it, a country that had possessed a deep tradition of religious philosophy at least two thousand years before the United States had been born.

Lal wrote that in a land of deep and subtle reli-

107

gious traditions, Billy and his message came up shallow: "The Metropolitan Indian Church . . . managed to convey the impression that a Prophet had come among them. But what the preacher delivered here, as elsewhere in India, was not what might be expected of a missionary of *real* stature."

Deciding to push an overwhelmingly unfriendly press aside, Billy took his crusade and his case to the people, the ones so diligently rolled out by the curiosity campaign and participating Christian ministers. Not realizing (or perhaps not admitting) that huge crowds will turn out for almost any event in India, Billy was overimpressed by the throngs that showed up for his rallies. Like a kid at his first major-league baseball game, Billy sent wide-eyed letters back to Ruth in North Carolina.

"Ruth, it was Wembley Stadium all over again! All you could hear was the tramp, tramp, tramp of bare feet and sandaled feet, as they were coming forward quietly and reverently . . . you could hear a pin drop . . . to receive Christ!"

The letters bristled with self-importance, ill befitting a humble servant of the Lord: "It was a very delightful experience. They had built a platform that almost looked like a throne, with . . . really . . . a crown on top!"

Billy reacted privately like a visiting colonial governor, with the "little brown brother" routine that had backfired so badly on the British when India rose up and booted them out in the late 1940s. Later, when portions of his condescending correspondence appeared in a book by George Burnham (a reporter from the Chattanooga *Free Press* who tailed the Crusade in India), the Indian government and religious community went through the temple roof. Billy was compelled to apologize publicly for his cultural snobbery. He promised he would never do it again—a promise he was destined to break, years later, in South America and Africa.

The preacher offended with more than his letters to the folks back home. During his circuit through India, he managed to commit every infelicity in the book. Rather than mingle with the masses during his free time, he relaxed in the villas and plantations of the upper crust. He refused to be physically touched by common people, even though their tradition teaches that such contact is a holy act of love and friendship. What's more, Billy had little time to sit down with Hindu leaders for the simple exchange of religious notes and ideas.

That reluctance to discuss and share philosophies was perhaps the greatest single failure of the India crusade. Billy could have tried to bridge the longstanding spiritual gap between East and West. He *should* have been keenly interested in the fact that Hindus and Buddhists looked upon Jesus as one of their own saints— an "avatar," or enlightened one. He should have set aside long hours with the holy men, to explore and expand the common threads of the great religions. He should have done all that, but he did not.

Perhaps he was only too well aware of his lack of education in philosophical matters, his lack of intellectual subtlety, and his ignorance about Hinduism and Buddhism. He must have known that he dare not expose himself to discussion and debate with men who would become aware of his shortcomings. It was safer to spend his time at the sides of swimming pools and upon the well-tended greens of English-owned golf courses.

Unfortunately, Billy's defense of his own ignorance was interpreted by the Hindu and Buddhist leaders as a snub. They had come to expect such indifferent treatment from Protestants in India. The only comfort came from the much better-educated Roman Catholic missionaries, who upheld a tradition of free exchange with the Hindus on both religious and cultural levels. The priests had always taken great care to adapt to the Indian way of life, not to remake it in their own image. Billy knew this, from the books he had read before the trip, but he chose to ignore the lessons the Vatican had to offer, or perhaps he felt himself incapable of meeting their challenge.

The Indian crusade came to a close in Madras on February 13, 1956. Billy departed for a whirlwind sweep of Formosa, Hong Kong, Japan, Korea, and the Philippines. In his wake, he left claims that eight hundred thousand Indians had come to the rallies and that twenty-nine thousand of them had decided to break tradition and accept Jesus as their personal and exclusive guru. Once again, a religious crusade had been reduced to tally-sheet statistics, most of which could not be checked for endurance or accuracy.

A turnout of eight hundred thousand was piddling by Indian religious standards. Many local holy men could do that standing on their heads, without benefit of public relations and government connections. Perhaps realizing he had suffered an international defeat, Billy Graham went home and left the preaching in the hands of Dr. Akbar Abdul-Haqq, a Hindu turned Methodist. Thanks to his lifetime knowledge of Indian culture and some on-the-job training at Graham crusades in America, Dr. Haqq became an effective evangelist in his homeland. He managed to undo much of the harm Billy Graham had done.

Beneath the Southern Cross

Billy didn't leave the States in 1957. His checkbook crusade in New York City provided more than enough hard work and headlines to keep him busy for the entire year.

But in 1958 he was back on the plane again for three weeks of public attention and suntan in the Caribbean. The result was even less impressive than the trip to India. Of the one million multihued island dwellers who showed up to see what was going on at the rallies, only twenty thousand bought the salvation sales pitch.

It was apparent that the law of diminishing returns was beginning to work against the law of God, not to mention Billy's best interests. Billy and everyone else on the inside of the organization decided it was high time to go crusading on a friendly continent, where Jesus and tent-show tactics were already built in to the culture. The perfect place was found "down under," in Australia.

Australia was the red-necked renegade of the crumbling British Commonwealth, the vast, frontier-fanatic and fundamental nation where a Protestant majority held sway over the likes of Catholics and boomerang-throwing aborigines. Australia had the same kind of nail-tough isolation and spirit of rugged individualism that had given birth to the evangelistic movement in pioneer, backroad America a century before. It was just what Billy needed for a personal, overseas rebirth in 1959.

To help the labor pains along, Billy's arrival on Australian soil was preceded by a full-scale promotional blitz capitalizing on the mass media. Throughout January and half of February, you couldn't turn the TV or radio dial without seeing or hearing some reference to Billy and his upcoming soul spectacular. Movie houses were booked long-distance from Minneapolis to run Graham-produced films like *Souls in Conflict*. Billboards multiplied faster than kangaroos in the Outback.

All the advance work paid off handsomely the minute Billy arrived in the southeastern-seaboard city of Melbourne, thanks in large part to Graham organizer Jerry Beavan. Beavan had moved to Australia in 1958, family and all, to scout the territory and draw the initial crusade plans. Armed with carte blanche to get the arrangements made, Beavan concentrated on arm twisting and money spending in the major cities of Melbourne, Brisbane, Perth, and Sydney. Backed by powerful Protestant leaders, Beavan lined up special landline broadcast relays and transportation networks to get the word out to the boondocks and attract as many people into the population centers as possible.

It was Beavan who urged Billy to expand the Crusade to four months, instead of the planned four weeks. He told the home office that the turnout was going to be big and that Billy would need preaching help from additional evangelists. Grady Wilson, Leighton Ford, and Joe Blinco were added to the roster, to meet the needs of Beavan's runaway agenda.

Beavan is also credited, in inside circles, with a stroke of pure psychological genius. He booked the opening Melbourne rally into a small, easily packed indoor arena. Although that first turnout was modest, it looked like a multitude when jammed under one deliberately inadequate roof. The Australian press played into Beavan's hands, remarking that many people had to stand outside because of lack of seats. The rest was left to human nature, as thousands of Aussies, thinking something must really be up, flocked to the succeeding rallies like gapers to a minor house fire.

By the end of the Melbourne stand, Jerry Beavan had moved Billy into the vast Municipal Cricket Ground. The climax came on Sunday, March 15, when

140,000 people showed up in response to the Gospel and Beavan's manipulation.

The same stampede tactics were used at every stop along the itinerary, throughout April and May. On a side trip to New Zealand, Billy preached to more than one-fifth of that nation's entire population. This trip was rated as the most successful six days in the history of his box-office-career.

On May 31, 1959, Billy waved goodbye to the friendly land of the koala and "waltzing Matildas," claiming that more than 150,000 sinners had accepted Christ.

The police magistrate of Sydney claimed even more than that. With a perfectly straight face, A. E. Debenham proclaimed that Billy's presence had cut Sydney's crime rate by 50 percent. Skeptics said that they doubted Debenham's figures were any more accurate than Billy's. Neither set of books was ever authenticated by anyone on the outside.

Bwana Graham: The Great White Soul Hunter in Africa

Flushed with the success of his triumph in Australia, Billy decided in 1960 to shed his light on the Dark Continent of Africa. Forgetting the unhappy lessons of the India crusade, Billy played benevolent *bwana* to the natives, while rubbing elbows with the leaders and clergymen of white-minority-dominated governments. For three months, Billy safaried his way from Liberia to Ruanda-Urundi, exhorting bewildered blacks to come out of the Stone Age, and into the modern church.

To no one's surprise—except, perhaps, Billy's—the audiences were large, but noncommittal to the point of

113

exasperation. Of 128,000 people who turned out in Lagos, Nigeria, during the week of January 24, only 4,500 came forth to sign pledge cards.

Billy blamed it on the language barrier and an unaccustomed lack of prior publicity. But a Nairobi newspaperman named Keith Dobson came a whole lot closer to the truth: "Graham came to black Africa expecting to find gullible heathens in paint and loin-cloths. Instead, he found human beings seeking their own identity and place in the community of nations. Like so many preachers before him, he never had an inkling that Africa had changed, and he had not."

To recover from his setbacks in the jungles and on the veldt, Billy concluded his African crusade with three weeks in the Middle East. He made a gaudy visit to Jerusalem, where he preached on holy ground and slept in the best suite in the King David Hotel. There were visits with Golda Meir, Abba Eban, King Hussein, and other ranking leaders on both sides of the Suez Canal. It was like a scene from George S. Kaufman's play *The Man Who Came to Dinner*. The hosts just had to grin and bear it, hoping Billy would finally decide to pack up his bothersome entourage and go home. On March 15, he finally did, allowing the Arabs and Israelis to get back to threatening each other with annihilation.

In the end, the African crusade had been as much a failure as the Australian had been a success. But for all of its disappointments, it did serve to keep Billy out of the United States for four months of the 1960 presidential campaign. This was part of Graham's deal with Nixon, to avoid having to make any political endorsements.

To keep his "cover" intact and his agreement with Nixon in force, Billy hit Europe in the late summer and early fall of 1960. The crusader stayed on foreign shores and beyond the reach of domestic political pitfalls. If he gathered a handful of souls in the process, so much the better for everyone concerned.

Thou Shall Not Drink the Water

On January 14, 1962, Billy plunged into the very heart of hostile Catholic country, with a brace of crusades in South America. The reception was so bad and the outcome so dismal that the four months spent south of the Border rate only two pages in *Twenty Years under God*, the fancy pictorial review of the Graham ministries.

For all his good intentions and press agentry Billy limped back from South America with an embarrassing twenty-two thousand converts to his credit and an undiagnosed intestinal ailment. Even though the unhappy memories of the Latin crusade went away by 1963, the bug did not. It laid him low on the very eve of a major invasion of Japan, Formosa, and the Philippines. He had to bow out of the Far East crusade and leave the preaching to Grady Wilson and other side men.

A newspaper editorial in Buenos Aires called it "poetic justice" and "divine retribution."

The Bible and the Big Screen

Spring 1970 brought a new and lasting dimension to the Billy Graham crusades: full-scale electronic impersonality. Borrowing a technique from American boxing-match promoters and George Orwell, Billy turned the Sawdust Trail into a closed-circuit television network called Euro-70. It was a spectacular the likes of which the European Continent had never seen, the spiritual "Wide World of Sports" in seven languages.

Planning for Euro-70 began in early 1969 when Graham accountants and staff crusade designers went

THE GOSPEL ACCORDING TO BILLY

to the boss with a problem. Overseas crusade expenses, they told him, were becoming prohibitive. The "cost to convert" figure was out of hand, and local fund-raisers were becoming less and less enthusiastic about bearing the burden of long-drawn-out revivals.

The challenge was simple: either shorten the international crusades and bring down expenses or face the prospect of going out of business. The problem was frightening, but the answer was already at hand, if only the bugs could be worked out: organize a multinational television and radio hookup for a hit-and-run crusade designed to reach the largest possible number of people in the shortest time.

Europe was picked as the target area, but not because it was especially in need of salvation. Practically speaking, it offered the best chances of success, because Billy was well known there, the region was already "Christianized," and the Eurovision Network was just sitting there, with coaxial cables and microwave relays ready for the renting.

As a dyed-in-the-wool media man, Billy loved the idea from the outset. He had experimented with it, on a much smaller scale, in Great Britain in 1966, with a ten-city hookup. It had saved him a lot of evangelical shoe leather and garnered him millions of dollars' worth of free worldwide publicity in the bargain. The technique had also worked in the second crusade to Australia (in 1968) and in several domestic revivals in the States. Billy brimmed with confidence and told his planners to get Euro-70 off the drawing board and on the air.

Billy's mandate was easier said than done, because it presented a new set of built-in problems that had not been encountered in the earlier electronic crusades. Those had been confined to relatively small coverage areas—English-speaking areas, at that. But Euro-70 involved more than one nation, more than one language, more than one set of technical specifications, more than one batch of local unions—and more than enough headaches, provoked by European political and church rivalries.

Billy's best organizers were put to the task, among them two Britons who had served Billy like loyal lap dogs in the triumphant past. One was burly-shouldered Harvey Thomas; the other was David Rennie, the television whiz who supposedly sketched out the Euro-70 network on a napkin one day while eating breakfast with Billy.

Harvey Thomas had his work cut out for him from the very start. It was up to him to get out and drum up financial and moral support for Euro-70 outside Germany. His boss, Walter Smyth, had already lined up the Crusade broadcast headquarters at Dortmund's huge Westfalenhalle. Armed with "salt money" from Minneapolis, Thomas tramped back and forth across Europe, looking for nations and cities willing to provide clearances and auditoriums for Billy's TV-relayed face and words.

After months of work and back-room bargaining, Thomas reported in with a list of nine countries signed, sealed, and delivered in the name of Christ and mass communications. These countries were Austria, Belgium, Great Britain (of course), Denmark, France, Holland, Norway, Switzerland, and Yugoslavia. Combined with sure-thing Germany, the total came to ten, a disappointing but final count.

For the public record, Thomas admitted that his search for nations had been a test of both his expertise and his spiritual courage. And although his results fell far short of BGEA goals, he gave credit to the Almighty for what little success had been achieved: "God did it! There's absolutely no other explanation!"

Divine intervention or not, Thomas and his staff of salesmen just couldn't line anything up in several countries where Billy Graham was considered less than a saint. The Swedes were as chilly as their climate, because of Billy's public protestations about their morals and their willingness to shelter American deserters. The Spaniards refused to open the door even a crack, because Francisco Franco detested being called a "godless dictator" from Billy's pulpit. The Italians turned a cold shoulder to the Thomas pleas because the Vatican told them to. And Soviet-bloc nations had nothing but party-line *nyets*, for obvious reasons. A well-founded rumor holds that Marshal Tito went along with Graham in Yugoslavia, just to miff the Kremlin in a new and different way.

Harvey Thomas's troubles weren't confined entirely to official foot dragging. He had plenty of trouble with European church leaders who didn't like the idea of getting involved with a "mechanized messiah." They still considered Christianity to be a doctrine of personal salvation, not a commodity or sport to be beamed out to the faithful on twenty-by-twenty-seven-foot theater screens.

To set their minds at ease, Thomas invited the skeptical clerics to Frankfurt in mid-1969 to enjoy an all-expenses-paid German holiday and to see the fantastic Eidophor big-screen projection system in action. The demonstration was a blatant sales pitch for the miracle of modern television technology. A number of British-based ministers were flown in for the occasion, to stand before the Continental doubting Thomases and endorse the techniques as if touting breakfast cereal. Reflecting back on their roles in the 1966 all-Britain Graham TV hookup, they said things like:

"This medium should be used again!"

"The great effectiveness was a pleasant surprise to many of us!"

"It surpassed all expectations, especially when we remember our initial hesitancy!"

"[It gave] a sense of oneness between the relay center and London!"

"The technician operating the projector even walked forward to commit his life to Christ!"

The timely Thomas demonstration worked like a charm, taking some of the sting out of his setbacks in Sweden, Spain, and Italy. Most of the churchmen went back to their homelands singing hosannahs to Eidophor.

While Harvey Thomas wrestled with the problems of church and state, Dave Rennie and his people grappled with thirty-six hundred miles of technical logistics. The biggest single problem was holding down the cost of facilities and engineering personnel. To help with that critical task, Rennie put more trust in the British-based Television Advisors, Ltd., than in God. But even the best efforts of T-A couldn't convince Eurovision or the European Broadcasting Union to back down from their materialistic ways. The people who ran those operations refused to provide anything free. Euro-70 had to pay cash on the barrelhead for every person and machine it used.

To offset that disappointment and broaden the coverage, Rennie and T-A horse traded with powerful Radio Monte Carlo to transmit the rallies by radio into eastern Europe, north Africa, and the Middle East. Combined with the ten-nation TV linkups, the radio transmissions made Euro-70 the most complex and costly closed-circuit enterprise in the history of Europe. Just getting it all to work at the same time was a testimonial to Rennie's organizational and technical know-how. But borrowing a public-image page from Harvey Thomas, he gave God all the credit.

A year later, in 1971, Rennie gave praise to the Almighty Technician in the Sky:

> *I spent quite a large percentage of time in prayer, even while I was working. In tight situations I would say, "Lord, it's way beyond me. If you want this thing to go forward to the glory of your name, you've just got to move in!"*
>
> *I suppose the evening I'll never forget was when it was eight minutes before the program was due to start, and we had neither sound nor vision lines. But panic was suppressed by prayer and it was remarkable that within three minutes everything was absolutely clear and ready to go.*

With that kind of holy control-room intervention, plus the salesmanship of Harvey Thomas and the cooperation and fundraising of more than two hundred participating European churches, Euro-70 went network operational on April 5. Giant screens flickered to life with the image of the leader, live and in full color from Dortmund. It was like *1984*, fourteen years ahead of schedule.

For seven nights in a row, the larger-than-life electronic evangelist drew them into the relay auditoriums. The message went to such places as a reconverted airplane hangar in Kristiansand, Norway; the opulent, gold-leafed Mozarteum in Salzburg, Austria; and the Saint Krizevcanin Church in Zagreb, Yugoslavia. They were vastly different settings in vastly different lands, but the final effect was the same. People felt as if Billy were among them in the flesh.

A Belgian friend of mine, who attended one of the rallies out of curiosity, later wrote to me with an eye-witness account of the spectacle. Going in, she had doubted the power of television over the human mind, but she left totally awestricken.

> *I had never seen so many people in the Centre International Rogier. I was compelled to give up trying to get to my reserved seat, and found a place close to the very large screen in the front. I had to bend my neck upward the whole night, which gave me discomfort.*
>
> *It was very warm for the audience, and there was some impatience because the picture and sound were not functioning properly at the start. An interpreter apologized to us in Belgian and Flemish, but soon the problem was corrected.*

My foreign friend was acquainted with Billy Graham through his other European crusades, but she had never actually seen the theatrics and staging of a real revival. She was a Catholic, accustomed to ritual, and felt that the Graham heavenly-host format was overblown and tacky. But she found Billy utterly arrest-ing—especially blown up to twenty-by-twenty-seven-foot proportions.

> *He was like a holy demon! He was all on fire inside, and his eyes seemed to be looking right at me like a giant cat looks at a small mouse. I found him to be very frightening and very kind, both at once.*
>
> *When he called for members of the audience*

to accept Jesus, many of them rose from their seats and walked down to the screen and knelt down to pray on the floor. It is the truth, Charles. They believed he was with them, and they reached up toward his face, and they were crying, some of them. I went home and told Mama and my sister about it, but they just laughed at me. Mama said no one would be so stupid to believe in a man on television—but I think she is wrong!

Mama, it turns out, was wrong on 15,813 counts. That's the number of souls that Euro-70 supposedly converted during the one-week life of the closed-circuit crusade. It was a new record for Billy—almost 830,000 people had seen and heard him within a seven-and-a-half-day span.

But Euro-70 provided the preacher with something more important than an impressive new record. Far beyond that, it served notice to his critics that he had not lost his appeal beyond the borders of America and that he could pack them in with pure imagery, scanned out of thin air and onto a screen.

With help from space-age electronic communications, he had found a way to sell the same old product, in a brand-new way, to a lot more people. Billy's closed circuitry and mass-marketing knowhow gave him the ways and means to spread the Gospel beyond 1970 and into a new decade.

He did it with a deep sense of evangelistic dedication and a much lower cost per thousand.

6

The Gospel According to Rand McNally

*No one ever went broke under-
estimating the taste of the
American public.*

—H. L. MENCKEN

If Billy Graham ever decides to hang up his Bible and
retire from the glory road, he won't have to worry
about getting bored or going broke. He can always keep
his mind occupied and pick up spare cash by going into
the domestic travel agency business.

Thirty years of crusading have carried him back
and forth across America, in and out of so many states,
cities, and motels that even his own expert statisticians
don't know how many millions of miles he has traveled.
Ever since Billy hit the trail in 1947, he's worn out more

sets of luggage than Elizabeth Taylor, Henry Kissinger, and the Harlem Globetrotters combined.

The list of the Billy Graham United States crusades is staggering, unmatched by any evangelist, living or dead. There are almost 140 of them on the list, encompassing well over 250 cities and a combined face-to-face and TV audience of more than seventy million. That puts Billy in the same league with Frank Sinatra, Ronald McDonald, and *Jaws*.

Interesting, Little-Known Facts About the Billy Graham United States Crusades

Most Visited Southern City: Charlotte, North Carolina—three crusades, three keys to the city.

Most Visited Northern City: New York City—three crusades but only one key to the city.

Most Visited Western City: Los Angeles—six crusades, six keys to the city, and one promise of a star on sidewalk along Hollywood Boulevard.

Biggest Single Rally: Los Angeles, Sept. 8, 1963; 134,000 at LA Coliseum; 20,000 overflow got bad seats at nearby Exposition Park.

Longest, Most Successful Crusade: New York City, May–September 1957 (sixteen weeks); 61,000 converts, minus Mickey Cohen.

Smallest Single Rally: Lihue, Hawaii, February 1965; 1,886 people, 244 converts, one Tahitian-style dance group.

Most Unsuccessful Crusade: Altoona, Pennsylvania, June–July 1949. The ten days Billy spent in Altoona were probably the longest and most embarassing of his public life. The turnout and response were so bad that the BGEA still won't reveal the attendance records.

Jealous Altoona ministers refused to cooperate with Graham organizers. Advertising and followup were nonexistent because Billy and his backers were broke. The crusade was so bad that even Billy's best friend, Grady Wilson, called it "the greatest flop we've had anywhere."

Most Financially Important Crusade: Portland, Oregon, July 1950. In Portland, Billy got the bad news that it would take twenty-five thousand dollars to get his "Hour of Decision" program on the ABC radio network. Since he already had a mortgage on his home and since his credit was bad in those days, he had to turn to God.

Billy prayed for a hefty heavenly handout: "Lord, I don't know where the money is, but it's up to you. I want you to give me a sign—twenty-five thousand dollars, *by midnight."*

That very same night (so the story goes), Portland sinners miraculously coughed up twenty-five thousand dollars into the crusade collection plates. To keep the money safe—and away from Internal Revenue—Grady Wilson kept the money in a shoebox under his hotel bed until a lawyer could draw up articles of nonprofit incorporation in Minneapolis. Once the papers were properly filed, the stash was transformed into the Billy Graham Evangelistic Association.

Thanks to Portland's generosity and God's timely intervention, the BGEA empire is now worth twenty million dollars.

Every Billy Graham Crusade has been touched by a miracle of one kind or another, whether instant money in Portland or a narrow escape from tar and feathers in Altoona. But, one of the biggest came along the garbage-strewn shores of Lake Michigan, in the nation's second city, Chicago.

Talk about miracles! It's one of God's wonders that the crusade ever came off at all.

Of all the cities in the United States, Chicago is historically the most salvation resistant. It sprang from the muck of a swamp to become Carl Sandburg's hog butcher for the world and the undisputed whorehouse of the midwest. Chicago gave us Al Capone, the Saint Valentine's Day Massacre, the Black P-Stone Nation street gang, and enough bagmen and crooked cops and public officials to keep a few honest prosecutors busy well into the twenty-first century.

As the old song goes, Chicago was and still is "the town that Billy Sunday could not shut down!"

In 1958, no one knew that better than Billy Graham. He'd cut his evangelistic teeth with Torrey Johnson in Chicago, and he was fully aware that the Windy City had buried more fire-eyed preachers than bullet-riddled gangsters. But Billy was in a gambling mood. With a successful 1957 New York crusade under his alligator-skin belt, he was willing to risk the long odds and give Chicago a try.

For all his zeal, Billy should have stayed home in Montreat and gone fishing with the kids. He couldn't stir up enough support to get even preliminary planning off the ground. Fate and Mayor Richard J. Daley were against him, as were the Chicago Church Federation and the gargantuan Catholic archdiocese. Billy Graham didn't have a prayer against odds like that—not in 1958.

At the very center of the "Block Billy Movement"

was the man on the fifth floor in Chicago City Hall. Dick Daley was halfway through his first term as absolute dictator, and he was dead set against having a non-Irish, non-Catholic headline grabber coming into his city to holler about its sins.

So the word went out, far and wide, to the right people: "The boss don't want this guy Graham makin' no trouble."

The Catholic archdiocese was first to respond to the warning, and not just for theological reasons. The church was just as much a part of the Daley machine as the ward-heelers who hung around smoking cigars at the Sherman House Hotel. No one, from the cardinal down, wanted a Protestant evangelist to make the city and its morals look bad. And no one wanted to cross the man in City Hall, for fear he might get mad enough to excommunicate them from the action.

The concept of separation of church and state was a local joke during the long Daley years. His power structure and patronage lists were overwhelmingly Catholic, and the City Council always seemed more than happy to cut through any amount of red tape to grant the archidocese special favors like zoning changes, building permits, and parades through the Loop. An act of kindness toward Billy Graham would have been suicide in 1958.

That same hard fact of life applied just as much to the city's Protestant leaders. In order to coexist with the Daley machine, the Chicago Church Federation played willing puppet. When Billy came to the federation seeking an invitation and sponsorship, the members just smiled and voted no. Only the renegade Moody Bible Church seemed interested in helping the Graham organization. But with the heat on from City Hall, the people at Moody had as much chance of getting a crusade rolling as they had of parting the waters of Lake Michigan.

Faced with insurmountable opposition, Billy retreated, like Napoleon, to fight again—perhaps when Dick Daley and his allies were in a more ecumenical mood.

But despite all the bad luck of 1958, Billy was heartened by his reception at Moody Bible Church. Both Moody and the BGEA stood to gain publicity and prestige by pulling off a major Chicago crusade, and both were willing to invest whatever money, manpower, and time were necessary to get around Daley and get the show on the road.

From late 1958 on, the Graham-Moody forces scoured for support in Chicago and the five surrounding counties. A small Baptist church here, an outcast prayer group there—the list of possible sponsors and fund raisers began to grow. By January 1962, it looked as if the dream of a Chicago crusade could be turned into reality, but *only* if a deal could be made with Mayor Daley. Since it was now self-sufficient, the proposed Graham revival didn't need the Mayor's blessing, just his nonintervention.

There's a popular though unconfirmed story around City Hall that Billy and his aides got on a conference phone line with Daley and his aides, to horse trade. Billy reportedly promised to go easy on Chicago's sins and shortcomings in return for Daley's promise to keep hands off and look the other way. As the story goes, Daley was impressed by the fact that Billy had backed off on endorsing Richard Nixon in the 1960 campaign. And since a favor to Jack Kennedy was also a favor to Richard J. Daley, the mayor agreed to let the crusade go ahead unmolested.

A number of ranking Daley watchers give little

credence to the story. They say it was not the mayor's style to grant favors to outsiders, unless he could bargain and browbeat them in person. These political doubting Thomases prefer to think that Daley felt secure in his second term and didn't see any further need to keep the preacher out of town. In 1962, with a Catholic in the White House and his local opposition totally neutralized, Daley really had nothing to fear from anyone—certainly not a street-corner evangelist.

Whichever version is true, Billy Graham suddenly found clear sailing in Chicago. And although the Church Federation and the Catholic archdiocese did not cooperate, miracles began happening left and right. The (secretly) pro-Daley media lent considerable time and space to the crusade preparations; the *Chicago Tribune* even arranged to publish Billy's sermons in full each day, once the revival got rolling.

More amazing, crusade sponsors had no trouble renting the cavernous city-owned McCormick Place lake-front convention center and the hundred-thousand-plus seat Soldier Field football stadium. The park district even promised to spruce up the stadium for the big event.

Scores of details that only City Hall could take care of were handled with uncommon dispatch. The Chicago Transit Authority came across with shuttle buses; the police department drew up special traffic-control plans; and the Illinois Central Railroad (an old Daley booster) okayed making Twenty-third Street a regular stop for all suburban commuter trains during crusade hours.

The stumbling blocks were removed, giving BGEA planners and promoters an open field. Billy was booked on every available radio and TV talk show, and arrangements were made to have him preach behind

129

the bars at prisons like Joliet and Stateville. Even the inmates at Daley's own Bridewell city jail were given a chance to see the preacher in action.

For added mileage, Billy's media men lined up 171 television stations in the United States and Canada to carry videotape of the last five meetings—the final full week of the scheduled three-week crusade. What had begun so badly, in 1958, now promised to be one of Billy's biggest and best-covered triumphs.

The Chicago crusade opened on the evening of May 30 as forty thousand people filed into McCormick Place to see the show and hear the message. Billy, of course, was at his theatrical best, playing big in a city that traditionally reserved its best turnouts for White Sox Sunday double-headers against the New York Yankees. But Billy didn't need the Bronx Bombers to fill the galleries. He did it all on his own. To his own surprise, and no doubt, the surprise of the Church Federation, McCormick Place was packed to its forty-thousand capacity every night of the revival's run.

Filling an air-conditioned convention hall was one thing, but getting a multitude to come out to the grand finale at Soldier Field was quite another, especially when the weather bureau predicted temperatures of 110 degrees. And that was the unpleasant prospect facing Billy on the last day of the Chicago crusade, Sunday, June 17.

They say hell has no fury like a heat wave in Chicago. It's an unbelievable combination of Death Valley and equatorial Africa—humid enough to mildew everything and everyone in sight, hot enough to make your eyeballs squeak inside their sockets. It's hardly a time to sit in the noonday sun, on a cement-hard bleacher seat, hoping to find eternal life. But that Sunday, 116,000 Chicagoans ignored the threat of terminal heat stroke, and turned out at Soldier Field to watch Billy sweat for their souls.

Billy played the sweltering heat to full advantage with an old Southern tent-show trick—divinely inspired exhaustion. He stood before the Soldier Field throng, bareheaded and brimstoning. It was Camille's deathbed scene all over again as Billy fought to keep from fainting, waving away assistance from appropriately concerned aides. An ambulance was conspicuously parked nearby, to drive the point home to the poor, sweltering devils in the distant seats.

Sweat-soaked and sagging, Billy remained superhumanly upon his feet until he delivered the familiar call to come forth. Then, while seventeen hundred heat-stricken converts stumbled down to make their personal decisions, the parboiled preacher beat a hasty retreat off the stage and into a waiting air-conditioned getaway car.

Back at his $150-a-day hotel suite, Billy sat on the edge of his bed in his underwear, fuming at aide T. C. Jones. Billy complained that the crowd had seemed listless and unresponsive despite his heroic performance. He bitterly remarked that the last big meeting had probably recorded more cases of heat prostration than converts.

Billy also told T. C. that he was worried about the videotape replay of the last rally. He feared it would look dull when it hit those 171 TV stations. Angered by his bad luck with the weatherman, Billy stomped off to his room with a tall, cold drink and left orders not to be disturbed.

At the very same time, in another part of town, Billy's music and staging expert, Cliff Barrows, had a full-scale panic on his hands. The editing of the Soldier Field videotape had run into a serious snag. The final program had come up seven full minutes short of its scheduled broadcast time. Barrows suddenly found himself in the middle of a four-way argument with a committee of Graham cronies over how to fill the seven-minute gap. Dick Ross, Walter Bennett, and ad man Fred Dienert insisted that the only way out was to sit Billy down in a studio the next day to fill out the program with an armchair minisermon. But Barrows was dead set against the idea, for fear it would come off like a weak programming afterthought.

The hassle continued for an hour or so, until the show-business lightbulb went off over Barrows' head. Let's send Billy back to the empty stadium *tonight*, he argued, to do the filler segment. Barrows' idea was like a godsend. The contrast between day and night was pure television drama, a network-quality show stopper. Ross, Bennett, and Dienert loved the compromise the second it left Barrows' mouth. They all agreed to ignore T. C. Jones's protests and get Billy on the phone.

At first Graham didn't think much of the idea. He was tired and still brooding over the disappointing response to his sun-baked matinee. Barrows, however, applied some practical psychology and convinced Billy that the seven-minute tack-on would save the tape—and the day.

Reluctantly, Billy put on his pants and dragged himself back to Soldier Field, scribbling out his remarks in the car on the way. When the preacher left Soldier Field for the last time, he was fully convinced that the day had been a total and expensive loss.

A week later, Billy found out how wrong he had been and how right Cliff Barrows had been. When the replay of the Soldier Field meeting hit the air over the United States and Canada, it triggered the biggest mail and telephone response in the history of the domestic

Graham crusades. The people in Televisionland loved the program, especially the marvelous seven minutes at the very end.

Just picture the scene on the twenty-three-inch monitor in your mind. The sweltering Soldier Field rally is drawing to a close, Billy has staggered away, screen left, and the crusade chorus wells up in song as the production credits roll. Then the chorus fades . . . and suddenly the crowd is gone and night has fallen. The camera pans down from the floodlit doric columns, to reveal a solitary figure on the empty stage, like Shakespeare's Hamlet talking to Yorick's skull.

Now the camera stops its pan and zooms in to fill the screen with Billy Graham's exhausted face, dark circles under the eyes. There's a dramatically timed pause, and then the soliloquy:

> *It's been three hours since the benediction was pronounced, and I have come back here to Soldier Field to talk to you. . . .*
>
> *The breeze is blowing. I think this afternoon was the hottest I ever preached on. . . .*
>
> *Some of you during this meeting have almost been persuaded to give your life to Jesus Christ, but you haven't done it. And as this stadium is empty now, your heart is empty; and yet Christ is willing to come in and fill it, to bring you a peace, a joy, and a satisfaction that you have never known before.*
>
> *You don't have to be here in this big stadium. There's nothing about the mechanics of coming forward that saves anybody's soul.*
>
> *But you say, "Billy, I'm really too great a sinner. I've just been too bad; I've done too many things. I'm too big a hypocrite." No, you're not too much a sinner. When he died on the cross, he was*

dying for you. He took your place. Your sins were put upon him . . . not just the sins of this big crowd we had today at Soldier Field.

The camera pulls back for a final, shadow-draped panorama of the stadium; then the screen fades movingly to black silence. Billy's four-year effort to save Chicago from itself slips into history with the drama and flair of a holy "Hallmark Hall of Fame."

The 1962 Chicago crusade—and the videotape rerun—was one of the evangelist's best performances, on stage and off. He had overcome a hostile reception, uncomfortable weather, and assorted technical difficulties in three headline-grabbing weeks. It was a monument to his ability to stay cool and calm in public, while all hell broke loose in private.

Had Billy been a Catholic, even Mayor Daley would have been proud of him. Who knows? The old kingmaker might have backed him for public office. Who knows? If Billy had been a Catholic, he might have accepted!

7

The Handy-Dandy, Easy-to-assemble, Do-it-yourself, Christianity Kit

Conform and be dull.
—JAMES FRANK DOBIE

If God had truly wanted man to be a free and creative thinker, why did he give him *Popular Mechanics?*

Give the average American the proper book of instructions, and he can accomplish almost anything, step by step, without batting a braincell. Merely insert tab *A* into slot *B* and make sure to match the easy-to-understand blueprint.

That's the "Do It Yourself" approach to life that helped make this country what it is today: a shining monument to flagstone-patio barbecue pits, five-hundred-dollar basement bomb shelters, and paint-by-number murals on the sides of Chevrolet vans.

All you need is an ability to follow the list of instructions, and the good life can be yours at wholesale prices. Turn a Volkswagen into a two-seat helicopter gunship! Wire your house against burglars! Earn extra cash in your spare time by mastering the elementary skills of brain surgery! It's as simple as applying to a pulp-magazine school.

If spreading the Christian word is your project in life, there's no need to fret or even pray for guidance. It's already available in handy kit form, from the Billy Graham Evangelistic Association. Just call or write the friendly folks at 1300 Harmon Place, and they'll be happy to help put you in the Jesus business with a half-scale Crusade.

As the BGEA advertising brochure puts it, "The world desperately needs to hear God's plan for salvation. It is to this purpose that we have dedicated our time, our talents, and every part of our ministry to challenging people to know Jesus Christ as their personal Savior.

"As Mr. Graham is only one man, he cannot fill requests from all who seek a Crusade. But through the preaching of several men associated with him, many areas can have a Crusade, with the same careful attention to preparation and follow-up, though on a smaller scale."

Translated into English, that means: Any bush-league town can have its own simulated Billy Graham crusade, with a simulated Billy Graham at the rental-service pulpit. Billy only works the big-league cities, where the donations are more plentiful, the sinners more sinful, and the media coverage more reliable and far-reaching. And that's okay, because small towns got

136

used to getting second best when Ringling Brothers stopped pitching their tent every time the locomotive needed water.

But even if Billy can't see his way clear to spending a few days bringing Christ to your little community, he makes sure that you can conduct your crusade in a manner befitting his nonpresence. Like everything else he touches, Billy's road-company revivals must be carefully organized and played by the BGEA rules. If you can't follow the instructions, you can't use the Crusade Kit, no matter how religious you are or how wicked your town.

To understand better how the revival game is played and how the kit is assembled, we need our own little pretend town, with its own little pretend problems and its own little pretend concerned citizens. Even though Gittleman, Oklahoma, doesn't exist, it's based on scores of communities tucked away in the tanktown section of the crusade files at Graham headquarters.

Gittleman, Oklahoma, first saw light of development in the 1860's. It grew from a tiny cattle town into a major stop along the Gittleman, Topeka, and Santa Fe Railroad. By the turn of the century, Gittleman had become the country's leading producer of two-man, nickel-plated ripsaws, and the population swelled quickly to twenty thousand.

Someone found oil on Elmer Dudkin's farm and by the mid-twenties the town could boast two banks, three schools, and eleven churches, all proper and frontier-fundamentalist.

Then, like everything else in Oklahoma, Gittleman was knocked flat by the Great Depression and blown away in the Dust Bowl. Half the town headed for California, while the other half stayed to starve until better times. Thirty years or so later, the better times finally came, when a major eastern company built a plant to manufacture hand-grenade pins on Gittleman's vacant outskirts.

The boom began again and has continued to this day. The population is back up to nineteen thousand, and the town now boasts of three banks, a savings-and-loan, four schools, a Dog and Suds Drive-in, and thirteen churches, not to mention plans for a genuine synagogue.

Gittleman is rolling all right, but the picture isn't totally rosy. Children are seen smoking cigarettes on playgrounds. A new one-thousand-watt radio station is filling the airways with acid-rock music. Blacks have actually been spotted within city limits after sundown. And the Gittleman Gardens Massage Parlor has long lines in front of it on Friday nights.

The good people of Gittleman are alarmed, and they turn to someone they can trust in such matters—the Reverend Bobby Joe Pious, pastor of the town's leading church, the Sooner First Baptist. Pious is more concerned than anyone in town these days, because his membership is drying up faster than the Big Gittleman River at drought time and the collection plate is gathering more dust than income.

In response to the citizenry and the wolf at the door, Preacher Pious skips turning to his Bible and goes directly to the source—a stack of Billy Graham pamphlets, hidden away for just such an emergency. He finds the address he's looking for and fires off a desperate Mayday letter to the BGEA Associate Evangelists Departments in Minneapolis.

Thus, God's work begins. A Billy Graham mail clerk steers the letter to a Billy Graham keypuncher, who feeds the Pious pleas into a Billy Graham computer. Within minutes a Billy Graham automatic letter writer spits out a "personal" reply, signs it with a Billy Graham automatic signature, and gets it into the afternoon mail. Along with it goes a ream of printed instructions, telling Pious exactly what he must do to launch his own bona fide, tax-exempt Gittleman crusade for Christ.

The cover letter is warm and friendly but businesslike. It tells Pious that just wishing for a Gittleman soul gathering won't get the job done. The BGEA won't participate in any kind of crusade until it gets an invitation from the leading people in the community. To make that task easier, Bobby Joe Pious finds enclosed a standard-form petition, provided free of charge.

The small print tells him that he can't just stand on any corner asking for any old signature that happens to walk by. Instead, he will have to hotfoot his way around town, collecting the names of every ranking business, civic, and church leader who is able to operate a ballpoint pen.

Of course, the Good Reverend complies, not realizing that he has become an unpaid agent of the Billy Graham field-intelligence squad. That's the team of BGEA experts that can look at a petition invitation and tell you at a glance whether a town is serious about supporting a crusade. If the names on the list are plentiful and important enough locally the BGEA commits itself to God's call. If they are not, the BGEA commits the petition to the nearest wastebasket and erases the preliminary electronic memory banks.

Luckily, Pious has done his work well, and Gittleman passes its first big test of faith. Everyone from the local Methodist minister to the city clerk has signed the invitation, and the BGEA looks forward to a genuine welcome. It also looks forward to a nice guarantee of bank loans, modest rental rates, and plenty of the necessities of crusading like extra-duty police, parking spaces, and free exposure in the *Gittleman Gazette.*

Now that the BGEA has accepted the town's kind and spontaneous invitation, it is time for the Reverend Mr. Pious's "great awakening." He receives his own copy of the "Associate Crusades' Basic Concepts of Organization," the four-and-a-half-page chapter and verse of who does what for whom.

"Each Crusade, of necessity, must begin and be carried to completion by the local churches. . . .

"These churches provide all personnel for the committees who will give guidance and direction for the weeks of preparation, including also the days of the Crusade and the extensive follow-up program."

Reading further through "Basic Concepts" and a heap of other supporting organizational documents, the Reverend discovers that he'll need a small army of local people and a truckload of donations to get the Gittleman crusade off the ground. The division of labor is unmistakably spelled out—the people of Gittleman will do most of the work and pay all the bills; in turn, the BGEA will provide a second-string evangelist and field-tested advice.

The first ally Pious needs is a good attorney. Under the terms of his one-sided pact with the BGEA, the Gittleman crusade must be properly registered as a non-profit corporation, in strict compliance with Oklahoma state law. (Render unto Caesar those things which are Caesar's and unto God a tax-exempt status.)

Gittleman's best-known lawyer, Bud Fixer, is only too happy to help the Reverend cut the legal corners, even though he may be little dismayed by some of the provisions the Graham people insist upon in the articles of incorporation.

Article III, Section D, for instance, clears up any

possible confusion over who has to collect the money and answer to the creditors if the books don't balance in the end. The local people must agree "to receive and disburse the funds collected for the expenses incurred for such items as publicity, auditorium and stadium rentals, Crusade materials, secretarial salaries, office rental, stationery, postage, telephone expenses, evangelistic team salaries, living expenses, and transportation essential to the success of the Crusade."

You don't have to be a Philadelphia corporate lawyer to know when you're getting stuck with all the grief but none of the rewards—not when you read what Bud Fixer is obliged to include in Article III, Section F of the Incorporation document. This section requires the local folks "to contribute to the Billy Graham Evangelistic Association the offerings received on the final two days of the Crusade . . . and to donate to said Association any remaining balance of funds after all expenses are paid."

Since the Gittleman crusade is planned for only a three-day run, the budget is going to be tight. That means Pious is going to have to shake a lot of money trees to keep his spiritual project financially afloat. And even if it should spring a leak and sink, Article Ten provides the BGEA with a certified public lifeboat: "In the event of liquidation or dissolution of the Corporation, whether voluntarily or involuntarily or by operation of law, the remaining assets of the Corporation shall be donated to said Association."

With the articles of incorporation finally in order, Pious is ready to put his own crusade organization together, with help from his Billy Graham crusade field representative and his portfolio full of guidelines.

The people of Gittleman are indeed lucky to be associated with a younger, dedicated BGEA liaison man like Doug Happyhelper. He's a former honor student from a major Bible-belt university with a degree in business administration, a Ford Pinto, a good-looking homebody wife, and two children with blond hair and reasonably bright minds. And even though Doug is based 250 miles away at the BGEA Oklahoma City field station, he's always eager to be of help, twenty-four hours a day, any day of the week. He even drives all the way over to Gittleman from time to time at Gittleman's expense, of course.

Doug is pleased with all the work that the Reverend Mr. Pious has done to get the Crusade underway. Bobby Joe has filed the incorporation papers in near record time and put together a nicely balanced crusade executive committee, a panel of the best-respected people in town, with each number carefully matched to the BGEA rules for local leadership.

The book says the executive-committee roster should number from fifteen to twenty-five people for efficiency's sake. Not wanting to look like a piker, Pious has recruited the full complement of twenty-five. He gets a gold star for maximum effort.

The BGEA strongly recommends that a ranking civic official be designated chairman, and Gittleman's beloved Mayor Franklin Fleshpresser has accepted the challenge. After all, reelection day is only three months away. Give the Reverend another gold star for knowing which side his political bread is buttered on!

With help from Doug Happyhelper, the Gittleman crusade executive committee is a lasting tribute to Pious and his ability to follow BGEA instructions. The Committee is split nicely down the middle, 50 percent local ministers and 50 percent local flock. And even though the Reverend awards himself a vice-chairmanship, he has taken care to follow Doug's advice and share his job and his title with banker Milo Moneygrubber. That's two additional gold stars, with an oak leaf cluster, for spreading the action around.

The first meeting of the executive committee is a huge success, complete with coffee, doughnuts, and nonstop sagacity, as only Doug Happyhelper can dispense it. He's come all the way to Gittleman to lead the chosen few in assigning working-committee chairmanships. To avoid bickering and chaos the qualifications for each key job are listed on handy BGEA Form XCC-1.

The job of arrangements chairman goes to Burton Brickbat, the man who's built half the new homes in Gittleman. He's the hands-down winner, because his qualifications fit the Crusade Handbook to the last detail:

"Arrangements Chairman: A layman who can anticipate the physical requirements of a public meeting. He must be sensitive to detail and able to administrate [sic] a project. A construction company executive or owner has often proved most capable if his personal schedule is flexible."

Since new housing starts are down in Gittleman—and everywhere else in the country—Burt Brickbat has more than enough time on his hands to case out meeting places and estimate how many bleachers to build within them.

The outcome of the counseling-chairman race is a surprise to no one. The job calls for "a minister with experience and concern for personal counseling." And Pastor Bob Meddler fills the bill. He's been poking his nose into the private lives of his congregation for years. No problem is too big for Reverend Bob. He's got a stock, Bible-based answer for everything.

The next chairmanship is nearly the most impor-

143

tant on the list: "Field Work Chairman: A man with wide contacts in community, civic and religious life and a good concept of *public relations*. He may be either a layman or a minister."

There's only one man for that job—Ronald F. Rotarian. By his own count, Ron belongs to every fraternal and businessman's organization in Gittleman County. He needs a part-time secretary just to keep his meetings straight. Not only that, but he's a lay minister in his own church and headed a public-relations firm in Ohio before he decided to drop out and retire to Oklahoma.

And so it goes for an hour and a half, until all the working chairmanships are handed out and the doughnut supply exhausted. The music chairman is an actual musician who believes in prayer. The prayer chairman is an actual minister who believes in music. The whole basic organization is shuffled together according to Hoyle, and by the time Mayor Fleshpresser gavels everyone toward the exits, the executive committee is off the drawing board and in full operation.

Lining up a Billy Graham-style crusade involves a lot more than renting a hall or pitching a tent and hoping enough people show up to be "born again." It must follow a BGEA battle plan to be fought along three absolutely strategic fronts.

First, the scores of little details must be coordinated. Billboards have to be printed, folding chairs borrowed or rented, dinners catered, and so on. Scores of things have to be done and services arranged right down to having someone clean up the debris after the last rally has come to a close. Burt Brickbat discovers he's working twenty-three hours a day just to keep his staff of volunteers even with the workload.

144

Second, the BGEA insists that every available Protestant minister and key layman get behind the Gittleman crusade in spirit and deed. Pious bangs his knuckles raw on the doors of his competition, in the hope of getting public endorsements from every recognizable Christian within driving distance of town square.

The third front of crusade preparation is the most important of all, because it's what the Billy Graham associate crusades are all about—*financing*. Without a guarantee of the green, even God can't make the BGEA come forth from Minneapolis to do battle with Satan and his lieutenants.

Gittleman is again fortunate to have the likes of certified public accountant Donald Donator as chairman of the crusade finance committee. He has a well-known knack for talking people out of money, and he already knows the Billy Graham contribution code by heart.

The rules are rigid but simple. They're based on more than twenty-five years of BGEA fundraising experience, and that's saying something when you consider that the Graham crusades have raised more money than all other revival organizations combined. Impressed by a record like that, Don Donator bends every effort to stick by the rules and the BGEA money-making time schedule.

A full six months before the crusade date, Donator begins phase one. Armed with a projected budget, he selects a cadre of fundraising captains and draws up a list of "sure-fire" contributors. Since charity begins at home, the BGEA recommends that the list include all members of the executive committee, the volunteer working-committee staffs, all ministers involved in preparations, and key church members who have been clued in on the big event. And don't forget the captains. They are expected to kick in too, as an act of fiscal good faith.

This is a difficult time for the captains, because they feel a little awkward about pitching close friends and co-workers for money. But crusade kit Memo FI-B sets all fears aside with some hints and tips on using Billy Graham pamphlets as an effective sales presentation:

"Study these [booklets] for ideas as to what to say. Include the 'we' spirit of co-operation. Encourage with reports on what the Executive and Finance Committees have already done. Be sure to ask for an *immediate* response—if not a 'gift,' a 30-day promise."

Donator and his captains get down to the task at hand but soon run up against committeemen and friends who don't want to part with their cash. A frantic call goes out to Doug Happyhelper, who just chuckles at the other end of the line and assures them that a preliminary cold shoulder is as normal as blueberry pie. Doug tells Don Donator to keep on pestering the holdouts until they cave in and cough up. A week of harassment usually does the trick, in even the most difficult cases.

The technique works like a charm. Donator and his people bang away until they reach the BGEA's minimum goal of one hundred initial contributors, pulling in about five thousand dollars—more than enough to cover the costs of office space, telephones, and the other trappings of a fully functioning bureaucracy. And there's applause at the weekly meeting of the executive committee as Donator reveals he's raised about 15 percent of the total crusade budget on schedule. It's time to begin phase two.

This is where the Gittleman Crusade begins sepa-

146

rating the men from the boys and the Christians from the deadbeats. Phase two is the all-out effort to get money from every member of every church in and around town. It's a big job, requiring more time and much more manpower. But the BGEA comes to the rescue again, with its Crusade Team Plan, a useful adaptation of the old U.S. Marine rifle-squad system, although in this case no one has to wrestle with a rifle or worry about enemy snipers.

Each of Donator's loyal captains is assigned six volunteer "solicitors," each of whom has been carefully screened for honesty, integrity, and Christian heterosexuality. Every captain is given a list of potential contributors and a donation goal of thirty-five hundred dollars. That works out to five hundred dollars for each member of each Crusade Team.

That's a lot of money to squeeze out of a traditionally tight-fisted town like Gittleman, but Doug Happyhelper refuses to be anything but optimistic. Three months before the crusade, he brings the teams together for the kickoff meeting—a locker-room pep talk, in every sense of the word. He exhorts the teams to stand fast in the face of cheapskates and never take no for an answer. He reminds them that God is on their side in this venture and that towns much smaller than Gittleman have made their money goals, with plenty of cash to spare. More sales-pitch pamphlets are distributed to the troops, and they go storming forth out of the trenches to engage in hand-to-hand checkbook combat.

By the end of fourteen weeks, the teams return from the field, with victory—and another 70 percent of the total budget—in their grasp. No one has fallen short of her or his goal. The team with the biggest total gets individual Billy Graham Living Bibles, bought at discount from the BGEA generals at rear headquarters.

Flushed with success and the encouragement of Doug Happyhelper, Donald Donator is ready to launch the third and final phase of the finance-committee blitz. He turns his crusade teams loose on the godless segment of Gittleman and its environs, the nonchurchgoers. The BGEA considers this the most difficult and least financially rewarding phase, because people who can't stand Sunday sermons seldom see much reason to help support and perpetuate them. Nonetheless, Donator is told to give it a try anyway, and he does, managing to wheedle another 5 percent of the budget from stingy apostate pockets.

The crusade is now only a week away, and Donald Donator is sitting pretty, with a balanced budget, just slightly short of the 100 percent goal. What he doesn't have in the bank now will be easily gleaned when the rallies begin, and the collection plates start passing through the audiences. For now, all the running bills have been paid and the ledger books put on public display for the benefit of skeptics and critics.

Keeping a good set of books is one of the primary goals of the BGEA when it gets involved with local crusades. Billy and his organization have always walked a narrow line with the Internal Revenue Service, and the boss fears an audit more than he fears eternal damnation. Woe to the folks in Gittleman if Uncle Sam finds even a nickel out of place. With all that in mind, Donald Donator has followed the BGEA Financial Policy (Memo FI-A) as if it were a new set of commandments brought down from the mountain:

"Because this Crusade is conducted in the name of Christ and the Church, and . . .

"Because there is a danger of criticism in the handling of funds, and . . .

"Because the Billy Graham Evangelistic Association has won the highest respect for its financial policy, we must do everything possible to uphold this standard. This is especially important in our area where all non-profit organizations are under close scrutiny."

Thus saith the director of associate crusades accounting. Donald Donator has nothing to fear. He has recorded every cent of income and outgo on easy-to-use BGEA financial forms. Everything is in order and in triplicate. With the crusade about to begin, the finance chairman is at peace with his God.

But with all this talk about raising money, we've somehow lost track of the man responsible for the crusade, the Good Reverend Mr. Pious. We left him six months ago, criss-crossing Gittleman County in his station wagon searching for ministerial support. Since he's a likable sort of guy, he's managed to talk thirty-two colleagues into at least considering an active role in the rallies.

Using his "Vice-Chairman's Crusade Guidance Portfolio," he has surveyed every church in the area, like an Indian scout tracking herds of buffalo. At each church he has solicited help from a volunteer represent-ative and armed him or her with handout literature for wide distribution. He discusses the crusade with each minister and backs up each conversation with a form-letter invitation (composed by the BGEA) to attend a series of ministerial orientations.

Pious finds it comforting that the whole process has been preprogrammed for success by the BGEA and that absolutely nothing has been left to chance.

At the big introductory dinner for ministers the dais tables are arranged to match a BGEA-mimeographed floor plan. The layout is designed to give the visiting clerics, their wives, and selected church laymen good seats, with plenty of elbow room and direct line of sight to the speakers' rostrum. The floor plan also includes suggestions on how many waitresses to employ and when the janitor should open the hall and close it.

The agenda for the evening is also provided by the BGEA. It includes such essentials as the opening prayer, the welcome, the dinner, the appropriate music, the introduction of local bigwigs, and, of course, the warm remarks from the crusade's Billy Graham-appointed evangelist, Sky Spellbinder. Sky is a predictable hit with the guests. He used to be a Ramada Inn circuit standup comic and Western singer before he found God and changed his wicked ways to follow Billy and Jesus.

The dinner is a soft-sell success, from Spellbinder's humorous anecdotes about his boyhood in Alabama, right down to the ice-cream-cake roll for dessert. The ministers and VIP laymen have been buttered up along with the biscuits, and they are more than ready for the hard-sell ministers' breakfast and seminar the next morning.

This is nitty-gritty time for Pious, the big payoff for all his hard work. If the ministers buy the pitch, he's home free with a fully and spiritually endorsed Gittleman crusade. If they don't, he stands a very good chance of winding up on the BGEA blacklist. But with Sky Spellbinder on hand to orchestrate the breakfast, Pious has nothing to fear but overdone scrambled eggs.

Spellbinder is the master of persuasion as he challenges the ministers to find fault with the concept and execution of the Gittleman crusade. He turns aside difficult questions from the floor with the skill and grace of a bullfighter, because like Billy Graham, Spellbinder works from a memorized list of stock answers to stock stumpers. A professional tap dancer never forgets the basic steps.

With their fears and reservations adroitly set aside, the ministers respond eagerly to the Spellbinder call to forget denominational differences and get involved—first with a generous gift to the crusade coffers and then with a promise to join the Pious team for an active role in the rallies. Pledge cards are signed. There's a short benediction. And the Gittleman crusade is stamped with a guarantee of success.

Finally, it's the big night, and even the threat of rain can't dampen the spirits of the sin-weary masses as they converge by car and truck on the Gittleman Memorial Auditorium. Mayor Fleshpresser got the use of the hall at tax-payer expense by leaning on the city council. Burt Bricklayer boasts he got three thousand comfortable folding chairs from his brother-in-law, the superintendent of schools. Chief Bullhorn is only too happy to have five overtime police officers on hand to keep the traffic from backing up. It's just his way of saying thanks for being named to the arrangements committee.

Spellbinder counts the house, and although it isn't exactly Madison Square Garden, it's the biggest single turnout he's seen on the road all year. Plenty of people have shown up in their best clothes, and that's a good sign they've brought some spare cash. Spellbinder makes note of another good omen—the audience consist mostly of money-carrying adults; there are few children.

As the house lights begin to dim, a certain magic touches the inaugural rally. From this point forward, the crusade is out of local hands and under the full, precision-timed control of Sky Spellbinder and his small band of BGEA assistants. They have a job to do and a schedule to keep, down to the split second.

The proper cue is given, and the Gittleman combined church choir falls silent as Mayor Fleshpresser rises to the podium to welcome the BGEA team and give the Reverend Mr. Spellbinder the key to the city. It should take no more than a minute, according to rally rules. The mayor is steered back to his seat on the stage, Spellbinder says a short thank you for the key, and Pious introduces the other members of the executive committee. The entire sequence takes less than three minutes, well within the BGEA's standard guideline of five minutes. Everything is going according to the script.

With the formalities efficiently out of the way, the real show begins. BGEA professional song leader Grantland Goldenthroat leads the assemblage in the short version of an old-time revival humn, "How Great Thou Art." The supporting chorus is enthusiastic, if somewhat off key.

Then, in rapid-fire order, there's a reading of scripture from a participating minister named Sneed, an invocation from Pastor Jones of the First Calvary, a solo hymn from Goldenthroat, an appeal for donations, another choral number, and a *prayer* for donations from none other than Bobby Joe Pious, the man who made it all happen.

Then a murmur sweeps across the hall as the great moment arrives. Collection baskets drift back and forth, filling deep with offertory envelopes, loose dollar bills, quarters, nickels, dimes, pennies, Gittleman Transit Authority bus tokens, and stray metal buttons. The spirit of the almighty BGEA is upon the people, and they dig deep to answer the call. Those who find themselves strapped by the demand are assured that they can take an empty envelope home, to be filled up and mailed to crusade headquarters, postage free.

In ten minutes or so the till has been totally tapped, and the salvation of souls begins. While the money is hustled into a back room for careful counting, the choir raises its voice in praise of and welcome to Sky

Spellbinder and his message. Borrowing from the style and the words of Master Graham, Spellbinder takes Bible firmly in hand and warns the multitude that Judgment Day is firmly set for a week from Thursday, and everyone had better make peace with God or plan on a one-way trip to hell.

Prepare ye now, the flailing evangelist warns, because the Red Chinese have the bomb, Egypt and Israel are almost at war again, and Lucifer is pied pipering the young people of Gittleman away to the music of Mick Jagger and the Rolling Stones.

By now, Spellbinder has the audience in a sweat, and a few people are already up on their feet, scrambling toward the aisles, so they can be first in line for redemption. Sensing the proper time has come, Spellbinder extends his trembling arms and beckons the growing throng forward, to make their decision for Christ—and to pick up registration forms and informational packets from wide-eyed, acne-stricken student volunteers. Almost two hundred new and renewed Christians stumble down to the stage, while the chorus roars through a jubilant hymn, drowning out the sound of the armored car as it heads toward the First National Bank of Gittleman with the night's proceeds.

Each night of the crusade is substantially like the first, with only slight changes in the message and the ministerial guests on the stage. But the order of events in the BGEA agenda remains unchanged—first the money, *then* the reward. No one gets eternal life and peace of mind without first kicking into the kitty. The appeal for funds is especially fervent on the last two nights of the crusade, because every cent is bagged and earmarked for Billy Graham's northland treasury. Sky Spellbinder is always at his very best in the stretch run.

Of course, all good Crusades must come to an end.

Sky Spellbinder moves on to his next stop on the Hallelujah Trail, leaving a handful of young staffers to mop
up the details of Christian conversion. For a week or so,
the rear guard will help Gittleman's new sheep enroll as
members of local churches. Names and addresses are
carefully recorded, so that the faithful may enjoy the
blessings of future mail appeals for donations to Billy
Graham.

And then, in a twinkling, Pious, Mayor Fleshpresser, Donald Donator, and the other concerned citizens
of little Gittleman find themselves back where they
started so many months ago—alone. Thanks to the law
and good luck, the local crusaders have broken dead
even on income and expenses. The two-thousand-dollar
surplus they made left town along with the last BGEA
field advisor.

But more than money departed when the big
revival slipped into memory. The evangelistic spirit dis-
appeared too. It's just what all those Billy Graham critics say in the newspapers and on television—when the
preacher goes home, the holy fire flickers out.

Of the nine hundred people who made their decision to accept Jesus on BGEA terms, only one hundred
still attend church six months later. Of that number,
only thirty-five manage to make it every Sunday. If
those critics are right, by this time next year, almost all
the converts will be sleeping on the Sabbath.

Worse, Gittleman doesn't seem much better off
than it was before the BGEA accepted the task of helping clean things up. Children are still puffing away at
recess. The acid-rock station is planning to expand to
five thousand around-the-clock watts. And the lines at
Gittleman Gardens seem to get longer every weekend.

And under pressure from concerned citizens and
the increasingly vacant pews in his own church the

154

Reverend Bobby Joe Pious is busy composing another letter, asking for another revival.

Since Gittleman, Oklahoma, has a good credit rating and follows directions so well, a second Billy Graham crusade kit will probably soon be on it's way, C.O.D.

If launching a full-scale Billy Graham–style Crusade is beyond your means or if your town is too far gone to hell to support a revival, there is still a way to find salvation, right in the comfort of your own home.

The BGEA invites everyone to send to Minneapolis for free literature and computer-composed advice on personal problems. Donations (the BGEA calls them "offerings") are welcome, of course.

If reading about salvation isn't enough to satisfy your soul, just tune in to Billy's own "Hour of Decision" radio program. Don't forget to send a few dollars along, if you enjoy the show.

Everyone understands that Billy Graham is a very busy man and cannot come to visit your home, even if you invite him. But thanks to the people at Grason Distributing (a BGEA subsidiary) up in Minneapolis, you can purchase a little bit of Billy at reasonable prices.

The full-color Grason catalog is a veritable treasure chest of Graham goodies, all available through the mail in return for your check or money order.

For instance, you can be the proud owner of Billy's bestselling books *The Jesus Generation* and *World Aflame*. Both tell you, in blood-curdling detail, about how the world is coming to an end and how you can get through the horror reasonably intact. If you buy both books from Grason, it will cost you a modest total of $8.90. If you don't mind paperback, you can get away for just $2.70—a darn good investment, considering that your immortality is at stake.

If you find that kind of reading a bit too heavy, but you have $3.95 to spend, why not ask Grason's to send you a copy of *Our Christmas Story*, written by Mrs. Billy Graham? The Grason catalog description of Ruth's work is compelling:

> Our Christmas Story *by Ruth Graham is not just another book about the birth of Jesus Christ. It is a unique account of the events that preceded and foretold the nativity of our Savior. Mrs. Graham has added a very personal touch to the narration by sharing with the reader the activities that take place in the Graham home during Christmas season. She cleverly carries the reader from Graham's front room, back to the Garden of Eden, where the journey to Bethlehem actually began.*

Grason's also offers a wide variety of religious volumes by other authors, with the Billy Graham seal of approval—such minor, modern-day classics as *What About Horoscopes? Demons in the World Today; A Foreign Devil in China; From Parent to Child about Sex; Let's Succeed with Our Teenagers; The Bride's Book of Ideas;* and *Casseroles I Have Known,* by the irrepressible Flo Price.

Of course, millions of misguided sinners among us don't like to read, and Grason's has thought of that too. For less than $20.00 you can order cassettes featuring selected Billy Graham sermons. A less-formal Billy Graham "rap session" is also available on cassette for the unheard-of low price of $4.95. You'll thrill to Billy as he sits with a group of young people and lets it all hang out on such timely topics as "God, Satan, Sex, Drugs, Marriage, and others."

Grason's also has a full line of inspirational long-playing stereophonic record albums that every Billy Graham follower will want to have. BGEA hymn master George Beverly Shea will sing you his favorites for just $2.50. Cliff Barrows "Presents Exciting Songs Along the Way" for just under $6.00. And the entire Billy Graham international crusade choir can squeeze itself into your Family Room for a bargain $1.95.

Last but not least, if you can't wear your spiritual heart on your sleeve, then why not wear a Billy Graham "love key" on a chain around your neck? The corrosion-resistant pendants are available through Grason's The keys symbolically open locked doors of communication—a likeness of Jesus himself is carved in the teeth. A matching scripture-verse key chain and a Billy Graham Bible memory packet can also be ordered for immediate delivery.

Next to the Holy Bible, the Grason catalog is probably the most important publication in Billy Graham's Christian world. With it, all things are possible. Just put your faith in the Almighty, Billy Graham, free enterprise, and the U.S. postal service.

8

The Preachmaster General of the United States

A civilian ruler dabbling in
religion is as reprehensible
as a clergyman dabbling in
politics. Both render themselves
odious, as well as ridiculous.
—JAMES GIBBONS

Throughout American history, men of God have passed in and out of the main gate of the White House with unfailing and much-ballyhooed regularity. It looks good for presidents of the United States to rub elbows with religious leaders, even if those religious leaders turn out to be sinful and ambitious in the end. And it looks good for religious leaders to rub elbows with presidents of the United States, even if those presidents turn out to be sinful and dishonest in the end.

Of all the divinely inspired Oval Office visitors in

159

this century, Billy Graham has knocked the loudest and the most often. Ever since Harry Truman packed up his piano and went back to Missouri, Billy Graham has probably done more laps around the Rose Garden than the White House landscaper.

That's heady stuff for a country kid from Carolina, even when he's history's most successful road-show preacher. It's heady enough to give him ideas about moving into the White House on a more permanent basis. And in 1964, that's exactly what Billy wanted to do. The only thing standing in his way was the awesome presence of a personal friend named Lyndon Baines Johnson.

It all began in midspring 1964. The weather grew warm in Washington, while Lyndon Johnson grew restless for full power. LBJ was already beginning to act and sound like his old wheeler-dealer Texas self and less like the humble steward of John F. Kennedy's unfulfilled plans and policies.

And while the real Lyndon Johnson blossomed with the cherry trees, millions of Americans began to realize that the nation was very much at war in a distant country called Vietnam. Although the nasty little fight had not yet grown to the national agony it was destined to become, Vietnam was an election issue in an important election year, and LBJ knew it. It was dawning on an increasing number of Americans—even a few generals—that you can't save a country by destroying it. Johnson assured the people that all he needed was some time and a ballot-box mandate to end the conflict and get on to more important matters like employment, equal rights, and integration.

Everyone who was hooked in to the political realities of 1964 knew full well that Johnson was going to run for a legitimate, four-year elected term. But no one had even the faintest notion who would have the guts and the backing to run against him. LBJ had the weight of his political connections and the momentum of his accidental incumbency, and they made him a vote-getting juggernaut of almost Rooseveltian proportions. At last he had the ultimate power in his hands, and he knew how and where to use it.

Republicans and outcast Democrats alike looked to their ranks and found themselves woefully few in number and desperately short of candidates who could turn things around and kick the tumultuous Texan out of the White House and back to the ranch.

The presidential pickings were so dismal that even right-wing Arizona Senator Barry Goldwater was being talked about as a leading contender for the main event in November. Even though Goldwater's hard-nosed pronouncements and silver-topped tan stirred considerable public interest, practical politicians considered the Senator too far from the comfortable American middle to wind up anything but clobbered in a showdown with LBJ.

The refugees from the JFK camp didn't find prospects much better. The surviving Kennedys, Teddy and Bobby, were far too green and much too close to the tragedy of Dallas to pose any real threat to Johnson in the 1964 convention. Party gunners, like the late Mayor Richard J. Daley of Chicago, figured that the Kennedy mystique would have to be kept in mothballs until at least 1968. More likely, the Kennedy kids would have to wait until '72, because Lyndon wasn't likely to call it quits until he'd served his full constitutional allotment of two complete terms.

If the prospect looked bleak for anti-Johnson Democrats, it was absolutely desolate for the tattered remnants of the Nixon movement. In the spring of '64, their

THE GOSPEL ACCORDING TO BILLY

man was the great American laughingstock—a shifty-eyed, half-shaven bungler who had debated himself out of the presidency in 1960, then managed to get pounded to a pulp in the 1962 California governor's race against Pat Brown. Nixon had skulked away to hide behind the heavy oak doors of a New York City law firm. And he would not emerge into the political light of day for another three years at least.

Briefly, then, there was no one on hand in 1964 with the flash, fire, and financing needed to defeat Lyndon Johnson. But in the midst of all his sure-thing confidence, Johnson hit a patch of rough road along the victory trail. Ironically, another big-name Texan provided the chuck holes and detour signs. Midway through May, millionaire conservative H. L. Hunt told the *Dallas Times Herald* that he was ready and willing to back the one man on earth who could walk all over Lyndon, and everyone else, to win the presidency.

Hunt proclaimed that Billy Graham could bring LBJ to his knees, though not to pray. The way Hunt figured it, the Prince of Preachers had more than enough charisma and popular following to be a big winner.

News of the left-field endorsement spread like wildfire, of course, variously baffling, electrifying, or amusing everyone who got wind of it. The pundits and the commentators couldn't resist the urge to speculate about the outlandish possibility of a Graham candidacy and what it might do to the American political process.

Corner saloons bristled with angry debates over real and imagined threats to the separation of church and state. Hundreds of clergymen mounted their pulpits, some to urge the evangelist to throw his Bible into the ring, others to warn him away with congregational petitions of righteous protest.

162

But for days, Billy said nothing, while a whirlwind of publicity blew some welcome attention in his direction. When Billy finally did step into the frenzy, he did it with typical flair and a bucket of cold water, the contents of which he threw upon Hunt at a brief meeting with reporters in Switzerland. Giving the Almighty the standard plug, Billy revealed that he had no intention of changing careers.

As he put it, "I have a much bigger job as preacher of the Gospel than any political sphere in the world. And I intend to continue preaching the Gospel as long as the Lord gives me breath!"

With those two short sentences Billy Graham made it clear that he wanted no part of Hunt's plan. A hard core of true believers nevertheless spent the rest of the year sending him letters, begging him to reconsider and to establish the Kingdom of God at 1600 Pennsylvania Avenue.

But, such was not to be. When election day, 1964, rolled around Billy was still a simple minister, Barry Goldwater was a household joke, and Lyndon Johnson was a full-term, landslide president—just as everyone had expected.

Now, on the surface, Billy Graham's role in the 1964 campaign was that of a well-known but innocent bystander. Those who accepted what he said in Switzerland reasoned that H. L. Hunt had simply gone off half-cocked, without ever asking Billy if he wanted to be president. Such crossed wires are not uncommon in partisan politics.

That was the way it looked on the surface, but the picture changes considerably a bit deeper down. In truth, Billy Graham was dying for a shot at the presidency, long before Hunt went public with his celebrated Dallas trial balloon.

163

A number of people who were close to Billy in 1964 have told me that their boss was constantly barraged by high-placed offers to give up the ministry in favor of a much more prestigious and powerful calling in Washington. They say that before Johnson made his final decision to run, Billy was beset by a host of politicians and businessmen who stood to gain quite nicely by a radical change of presidential leadership. H. L. Hunt was only one among many who were willing to roll the dice in the hope that Billy would be willing to gamble along with them.

Billy listened to the offers closely and spent a good many long days and sleepless nights mulling them over. There was secret talk of converting the Graham crusade machinery into an orchestrated grass-roots campaign organization. Lists of possible endorsements were drafted, and numbers of experts were called in to estimate just how many donation dollars it would take to launch and sustain a nationwide "Billy for President" blitz. The nuts and bolts of a serious White House bid were assembled behind closed doors, and it was soon up to Billy alone to give the signal for go or no go. Faced with that ultimate and frightening decision, Billy turned on his backers and piously bailed out of the arrangement.

But Graham's retreat was not based on his fear of the wrath of God. A ranking defector from the Graham organization says Billy wrestled more with political practicalities than with his conscience. Billy knew that he didn't have the stamina or the knowhow to defeat Lyndon Johnson in a real campaign showdown. He was an LBJ crony, properly awestricken by the president's ruthless and uncanny knack for tearing the jugular out of his opponents.

Billy was not prepared to expose his throat to such

a dangerous adversary. Nor was he willing to expose his private life to the media glare of a presidential campaign. Beneath his warm, confident, spellbinding on-stage personality, Graham was and is plagued by self-doubts and a near-crippling terror that outsiders will burst through his public façade to discover and reveal his private self. He feared that a bid for the presidency might leave him open to questions he could not answer and probes he could not turn aside.

Still another factor weighed heavily in the decision: Billy was afraid to loosen his control over his own multimillion-dollar evangelical empire. It had taken him years to build it into a ministerial and financial power center, and to leave it in other hands was unthinkable. Billy didn't want to risk his life's work against the poor odds in favor of beating Lyndon Johnson. Even if he somehow did become president, he would not be even remotely prepared to divest himself of all he had going for him in Minneapolis and out on the crusade trail. He had direct control of the biggest single money-making religious organization outside the Vatican walls, and not even the promise of being president could make him let go.

In the years since Billy Graham made his personal decision to stay full-time with Christ, he has never been seriously mentioned again as candidate for president, although plenty of Hunts around the country still like the idea. Rather than possess the power of the presidency, he has been content to just be near it, feel it, and have it rub off a bit on his ego and image.

For a generation, he has courted and collected U.S. presidents like charms on a bracelet. Graham's compulsion to sit in the very inner circle of high-echelon politics overwhelmed him during the dying days of America's most flamboyant and influential administration.

FDR and Hard-hearted Harry

Graham's first encounter with a United States president was hardly anything to write home about, although that's exactly what he did, in great and excited, though exaggerated, detail. The meeting amounted to a two-second handshake with Franklin Delano Roosevelt during a mid-1940s gathering of young churchmen in Washington, D.C. Billy was a virtual nobody then, just another green preacher who wasn't sure if he wanted his own flock or a life on the evangelical circuit.

The country boy in Billy was deeply impressed by both FDR's presence and his life-style, and the young preacher made a promise to himself that he would return to the White House someday, not just to shake hands, but to stay on awhile, as an honored guest.

Slightly more than a half decade later, in 1950, Billy did come back, but this time he had the backing of the powerful Hearst newspaper chain, a reputation as a biblical boy wonder, and a burning desire to get on the good side of Roosevelt's hell-fire successor, Harry S Truman.

This time, Billy walked up the steps as the very center of attraction, decked out like a *nouveau-riche* rube, in an ice-cream-white suit, white buckskin shoes and a God-awful hand-painted tie that still remains a legend in political fashion circles. The outfit obviously fell well below the standards set by Harry the ex-haberdasher, but the press photographers loved it, and Billy loved their bulb popping.

He was every inch a gaudy spectacle on that July 14, 1950, when he waved and smiled at the newsmen, then ducked inside to meet America's best-known caustic host.

In those days, visiting Harry Truman was like

jumping into a tiger's cage at feeding time. You never knew if you would walk out alive. But remarkably, Billy found Harry in a pretty good humor. Harry even stood up and came around the desk to shake hands.

Harry Truman was a very fair, decent, and understanding man, and although no one has ever accused him of being religious, he was usually tolerant of those who were. He treated them with polite, distant respect. That little-publicized virtue even applied to headline-loving whippersnappers like Billy Graham. For a full twenty minutes (five more than the customary visiting time), Harry played the pleasant host to his over-dressed caller. He even endured a short, embarrassing kneeling prayer at the end of the chat.

The Truman audience was an unqualified success for Billy until he walked back out into the less exalted world and committed what most people agree was the biggest sin of his public-relations career. Rather than say no to reporter requests for details of the meeting, Billy told all. He even got down on the ground, like a zoot-suited back-alley crap shooter, to show how he and the president had hit the deck to pray for guidance and understanding.

The next day, newspapers across the length and breadth of the land ran the pictures, along with amazing accounts of how the young backwoods minister had somehow reached out and warmed the icy soul of the old devil in the White House. Banner headlines elevated the brief Truman-Graham gab session to a modern-day religious miracle.

When Truman read the newspaper accounts at breakfast, he went through the ceiling with a rage that he normally reserved for the likes of Joseph Stalin, Walter Winchell, and critics of his daughter's singing voice.

THE GOSPEL ACCORDING TO BILLY

Truman felt, rightly, that he had been used to further Billy Graham's publicity-laden career. And Harry used every obscenity at his able command to let those within shouting or phoning distance know about it. White House aides recall that the tirade lasted, on-and-off, for the better part of a very uncomfortable week, until the president came up with a punishment befitting the crime. He issued a strongly worded standing order that Billy Graham was to be crossed off the presidential guest list and banished from the building forever.

Word of Harry's tantrum got around Washington fast, and Billy soon discovered the magnitude of his bad judgment. Democratic welcome mats vanished faster than a Capitol Hill snowfall, and the embarrassed preacher found himself locked out of an entire administration just as surely as he had been locked out of the presidential mansion.

For the rest of Harry Truman's stint in office, the name *Graham* was nowhere to be seen or heard within a mile of the president. Even Harry kept his mouth publicly shut about the affront, until he went back to Missouri to play retired private citizen and vent his spleen in several volumes of remarkably candid personal memoirs. That's when Harry told the world exactly how he felt about Billy and his doorstep news conferences.

At the very best, said Truman, Billy was just another street-corner, Bible-banging fraud, with a following of fools who would probably be better off as atheists. To put it in more Trumanesque terms, the man in the hand-painted tie was "a phony son of a bitch."

Mr. Sid and General Ike

But in early 1952, the outcast evangelist was given a unique chance to help carry out Harry's eviction and help carry in the luggage of a new administration, thanks to a somewhat manipulating Texas tycoon named Sid Richardson.

"Mr. Sid," as he liked to be called by his friends and enemies alike, was a man to be reckoned with, no matter where your scruples or politics lay. He held the strings on every smart politician, influence peddler, and influence seeker in the Lone Star State. He was known as a crude and ruthless backroom slugger who could fix you for life if he liked you—or fix you for good if he didn't. Billy Graham was lucky enough to find favor in Mr. Sid's eyes.

The Richardson-Graham connection was made during one of Billy's very first crusading forays into Texas. Sid was impressed by the young man's good looks, flashy style, and ability to sell big to the masses. Richardson was a good judge of horseflesh, human or otherwise, and he considered Billy a hot prospect for nationwide success and power. Talk soon began to spread that mighty healthy chunks of Richardson's money were being laundered and delivered to the fast-growing Graham organization. When he wasn't helping God's work financially, Sid was busy introducing Billy to other young "comers" in the Richardson Ranch bunkhouse. Among them were Lyndon Johnson and a brash, ambitious lawyer by the name of John Connally.

Mr. Sid told Billy that both men would rise one day to rule the nation. And Billy told Mr. Sid that he agreed—Lyndon and John would make splendid presidents.

Of course, if you accepted friendship and favors from Sid Richardson, you were expected to repay the kindness, upon demand, without a blink of hesitation. In 1952 Sid came to Billy with an important IOU clutched in his fist. He wanted his spiritual protégé to sit down and fire off a letter to none other than General

of the Army Dwight David Eisenhower, and help convince the great warrior it was high time he got up off his
laurels and ran for president.

True to the Richardson code of the West, Billy
complied eagerly with the "request," prompting some
in-the-know skeptics to suggest that Sid had added a
new puppet to his power-brokering Punch and Judy
show. Billy denied it all, of course, and never more
righteously than in the pages of *McCall's* magazine, in
1964, a full twelve years after the fact.

Referring back to his discussion with Richardson
about the "Dear Ike" letter, Billy regaled *McCall's* readers with a slightly self-serving scenario, complete with
dialogue:

> BILLY: *Mr. Sid, I can't get involved in politics!*
> MR. SID: *There's no politics, Billy. Don't you think
> any American ought to run if millions of people
> want him to?*
> BILLY: *Yes, Mr. Sid. I agree he should.*
> MR. SID: *Well then, say that in a letter!*

The fact that Sid Richardson never did anything
nonpolitical in his adult life makes the Graham account
a little hard to swallow. It's also difficult to believe that
Sid could get through a conversation without swearing
at least once. But no matter what was really said to
whom, General Eisenhower got his letter from Billy, in
return, Billy got some important recognition from General and then President Eisenhower.

Billy described the wonder of it all, a bit further
down in the *McCall's* article:

> *I added my letter to the many Eisenhower
> undoubtedly received. Mr. Sid told me later that
> the General asked him, "Who was that young*

> *preacher you had write me? It was the darnedest*
> *letter I ever got. I'd like to meet him some time."*
> *So Mr. Sid arranged it. We met at the Gener-*
> *al's headquarters near Paris. The General was even*
> *younger-looking and more charming and more*
> *down-to-earth than I had anticipated. He immedi-*
> *ately put me at ease, relating some of his past*
> *experiences and asking me what message I was*
> *preaching. . . . He listened very intently.*

The word *intently* hardly does justice to Eisenhower's
interest during that Paris chat, because he was desperately in need of religion to help his still unannounced
presidential bid. The general was a soldier, not a
churchgoer. And his backers were justifiably fearful
that unless he started sitting in a pew every Sunday, the
voters would never let him sit in the Oval Office the rest
of the week.

Enter Billy Graham to help convince a lot of
people that the old soldier was soon to be reassigned to
God's own headquarters staff.

Billy recalled,

> *The next time we met, he was Candidate Eisen-*
> *hower. When I handed him a small red Bible as a*
> *gift, he indicated he was disturbed by implications*
> *that he was not a religious man. He had already*
> *explained to the public that he had never joined a*
> *church because of the uncertain nature of his mili-*
> *tary assignments.*
>
> *"I won't join one during my candidacy," Ike*
> *insisted, "because people will think I'm doing it for*
> *votes. But win or lose in November, I'm going to*
> *join a church."*

Although that conversation was held in private, the
heartwarming details of Ike's prodigal-son promise

171

somehow leaked out into the open, where potential voters could be amazed and impressed. Whether the Eisenhower people let the cat conveniently out of the bag or left that job up to the Graham publicity pipeline is really not important. The leak had the desired effect —it made it look very much as if God and Billy and the Holy Spirit had touched and endorsed the Republican candidate.

The gambit went beautifully in Peoria and the rest of Middle America. And with Middle America in his back pocket, Ike steamrollered over an unusually intelligent but bewildered Democrat named Adlai Stevenson, to claim the highest office in the land. To the shock of no one, Billy Graham steamrollered right along with Ike.

While Harry Truman scowled and snarled through the final days of his beleaguered administration, Billy was off to share officers' mess in Korea with Ike's son, Major John Eisenhower. The two men spent Christmas day together, in full view of the newsreel photographers, not to mention thousands of half-frozen American troops, all trying to stay alive long enough for the president-elect to make good on his campaign promise to pull the plug on the totally useless war.

No sooner had Billy got back from his goodwill tour of the front lines, than he was summoned to New York City to huddle with Eisenhower and his inner circle. In a scene reminiscent of an old-fashioned fraternity pledge-bidding session, Billy was offered a place on the Eisenhower team, as religious consultant for the upcoming inaugural ceremonies. Billy later looked back on the meeting, in dramatic detail:

> *I delivered to him some snapshots of his son in Korea. As we chatted, he suddenly walked to the*

window and looked out over the city for a long time. His spirit was obviously heavily burdened.

Then he told me of his desire to set a moral example for the nation, and he said he would like to bring something spiritual into his inauguration ceremony.

I said, "General, you can do more to inspire the American people to a more spiritual way of life than any man alive."

We reviewed several appropriate Bible passages. Some writers have speculated that the [inaugural] prayer was prompted by me. This is not true. The idea was his own.

You can take Billy's word on that, if you are also willing to ignore all the evidence that Eisenhower had precious few ideas of his own during his campaign. Most postmortems on the "I Like Ike" movement reveal that the general was astoundingly ill-equipped to handle political strategies and that his big backers and hand-picked aides called the shots and shaped the image.

Ike may have liked the idea of attaining a state of grace, but it's doubtful he was the first one to think of it. It's equally doubtful that the celebrated non-church member sat down to thumb through the Bible for the right words to put into his inaugural speech. If he had, there would have been no good reason to drag Billy Graham all the way to New York to thumb along with him.

The inaugural, of course, was a huge success, the first ever covered on nationwide television. Eisenhower rode through Washington exuding fatherly courage and confidence and waving the new fashion sensation of the Republican business world, the Homburg hat.

Ike's address to the people was less than spellbinding, but the biblical passages did hold a dignified and only slightly overblown promise of better things to come. Better things for a country wearied by the stalemate in Korea, the anxieties of the cold war in Europe, the fears of internal Communist conspiracies, and the high cost of groceries at the supermarket. With Dwight David Eisenhower as commander-in-chief, everyone was going to be better off than ever before—everyone including the Reverend William Franklin Graham, who sat in the inaugural reviewing stand grinning just as widely as the new president.

The optimism of Ike's big day quickly dwindled away into eight years of national hibernation. The Eisenhower years were an era of mediocrity in which the foreign and the domestic scene got neither much worse nor much better. It was a time for just about everything wrong with America to ferment and fester—the two-term calm before the storm that was destined to break with Ike's departure and the arrival of the turbulent sixties.

But lackluster or not, the years between Harry Truman's ill temper and Jack Kennedy's Camelot were golden, busy ones for Billy Graham. Not only was he a welcome and regular guest of the Eisenhowers, but his crusades grew bigger, better, and more profitable, both in the United States and overseas. The Billy Graham Evangelistic Association turned multimillion and diversified. Billy himself went multimedia on a scale that no one could have remotely imagined at the beginning of the decade.

Although Billy constantly denied it and Norman Vincent Peale refused to believe it, Graham soon came to be looked upon as a unofficial White House chaplain. He ministered to Ike's needs in the presidenial quarters, at state dinners, and even on the golf course.

At the administration's request, Billy set up the first in a long series of White House prayer breakfasts and put together the agenda and the menu for the kickoff meal. He even had a say about who would be invited to the breakfasts. And when he couldn't be in Washington to preside, Billy often picked his own clerical replacement, to sit at center platform and pass the word of the Lord along like a stack of buckwheat cakes.

Eisenhower often admitted that he consulted with Billy on personal problems, although neither he nor the preacher ever revealed their nature. It is also well-known that Ike felt perfectly free to call upon his young counselor when problems arose on the job.

For example, there was the time the president was stuck with serious racial trouble in Little Rock, Arkansas. Should he send troops in to reestablish the law of the land or should he back off and let Governor Orville Faubus have his red-necked way? Ike asked for Billy's opinion. Billy told him that Faubus was a paper tiger. The troops were dispatched.

Of course, Eisenhower's reliance on the Graham expertise was not solely confined to domestic troop movements. Toward the end of his first term, the president was under heavy fire from members of his own party to dump Richard Nixon and accept a new vice-president on the 1956 ticket. Badgered from within and without, Ike dialed North Carolina and again asked for Billy's opinion.

Since Nixon and Billy were close friends, the answer was predictable. Good friend Billy insisted that good friend Dick was still every inch a political asset and should be kept. Nixon ultimately was kept, despite some angry howls from the back rooms in the GOP hierarchy.

Four years later, Eisenhower bent Billy's sympathetic ear with another agonizing question about his vice-president. Would Nixon be able to win, and then handle the presidency? Billy assured the worried chief executive that the nation couldn't survive without Dick Nixon calling the shots.

Ike and the 1960 Republican convention agreed with Billy, hoping that Jack Kennedy's Catholicism and lack of experience would somehow put Nixon over the top. But, when those hopes were narrowly shattered at the ballot box, Billy found himself swept out the door with the GOP, just as surely as if Harry Truman had returned.

JFK and Camelot

Actually, the Kennedy years were not that bad for Billy, from a public-relations point of view. He was invited to chat with Kennedy from time to time, and both men did appear together cordially at a number of public functions in full view of the nation.

But actually, Kennedy and his clan didn't care much for Billy Graham and certainly had little use for Baptist counseling in a staunchly Catholic White House.

There was more than just a simple religious difference between Jack Kennedy and Billy Graham: there was political "bad blood," as well. Early in October of the 1960 presidential campaign, Billy returned home between overseas crusades with a personal problem. He wanted to say something nice about candidate Richard Nixon, but he didn't want it to look like a full endorsement. Billy was struck between the need for neutrality and loyalty to his favorite Republican standard bearer.

Henry Luce, the powerhouse publisher of *Life* magazine, came to the rescue. During a personal chat, Luce suggested that Billy sit down and write a nonpartisan but pro-Nixon article for *Life*. He guaranteed there was plenty of space available in the upcoming issue, scheduled to hit the newsstands two weeks before election day.

Billy took the Luce offer to heart and fled to Montreat, where he batted out a quick hosanna to Nixon. Luce loved it and ordered the boys in the Linotype room to rush it through, with Billy's byline. Luce knew he had a potential political bombshell on his hands, one that might generate enough extra votes to put Nixon over the top. And putting Nixon over the top was very important to Henry Luce in 1960.

It was important to the Graham organization too, but not so important that they could let their boss get caught in the middle of a last-minute political shootout. Advisors came down hard on Billy, begging that he come to his senses and ask Luce to keep the article out of print. Even Ruth and Tennessee Governor Frank Clement badgered Billy until he gave in and called Luce at home, seeking reprieve. But the publisher remained adamant—the Graham indiscretion would run in *Life*, as scheduled.

Billy was in a panic now. It was time to call upon God for help; "On Thursday night, the night *Life* magazine goes to press, Ruth and I got on our knees and prayed, 'O God, if it is not your will for this article to go —stop it!' "

The Almighty responded that very same night, by tipping Kennedy press aide Pierre Salinger to what was going on in the Time-Life print shop. Salinger got wind of the Graham article through a Luce double agent and hit the alarm bell. Senator Kennedy exploded with an understandable rage and called Luce direct, with a plain-language demand that the article be burned and buried.

Luce was on the spot. Fearful that Kennedy might just win the election and then get even, he reluctantly ordered "Billy's Folly" dropped. Billy was beside himself with joy when the unhappy publisher gave him the news: "Mr. Luce, I'm so relieved I feel like shouting!" Though the public never saw the article, Billy never quite got off the hook with Kennedy for writing it. JFK held the grudge throughout his remaining life.

Privately, the young president gritted his teeth every time he found himself in Billy's beaming proximity, and aides took great care to discourage too many requests for visits. Brother Bobby detested the Graham flair for dramatics and is said to have done a remarkably good imitation of Billy preaching from the pulpit. First Lady Jacqueline Kennedy found it painfully difficult to lower her Brahmin standards enough to feel comfortable when Billy and Ruth came calling. Kennedy insiders say she treated them like poor relations from down the road.

The Kennedy life-style was geared for the best and the brightest of America's New Frontier, and not for the likes of a reconverted Fuller-brush salesman. And from 1960 until JFK's death, Billy Graham found himself tolerated but never accepted by the president.

As consolation, Billy stayed as close as possible to JFK's equally shunned vice-president, playing a long-shot hunch that his old friend Lyndon Johnson might get lucky and fight his way to the top in 1968. When a cruel twist of fate in Dallas cut short the wait of both men by five full years, Billy found himself assured of unprecedented access to the very center of American political power. What Sid Richardson had brought together back in Texas, no man could now put asunder.

LBJ and the Preacher

If you dig around a bit, you begin to understand why Lyndon Johnson and Billy Graham turned out to

178

be friends. They had similar roots and similar ambitions, not to mention like-minded tastes, styles, and hangups.

Both men grew up under a Southern exposure—close to the soil but not poor enough to have it rub off on them permanently. Both had successfully found the way to substitute guile and timing for blood, sweat, and tears and to survive the Depression years.

Perhaps even more significant, Lyndon and Billy shared the same down-home brand of evangelistic zeal. Billy got his by choice, but LBJ got his by heritage. Great-grandfather Baines had been a fire-and-brimstone circuit preacher of local note around Texas and had passed two conspicuous gifts along to his lively descendant. One was a flair for flamboyant speech; the other was a set of equally flamboyant floppy ears. Each was as well-known and remarked about as the other.

In their separate ways, Johnson and Graham grew up to become soap-box personalities. While one windmilled at a tent-show pulpit, the other dictated from the podium of the senate. Both men built their careers around being the center of attraction. Their inner urge was to manipulate and dominate the minds and actions of other men. They did it with skill and remarkable success.

Sid Richardson had been right when he tagged LBJ and Billy for greatness. They were natural-born power brokers who possessed that certain con man's gift for spotting the weaknesses in others and exploiting them profitably to the hilt. Both men knew the rules of the game through instinct, and the Sid Richardsons only supplied the opportunities and the right connections to help the instincts develop into full-blown public characters.

And as the Johnson and Graham characters emerged through the thirties, the forties, and into the

179

fifties, the men who possessed them grew steadily and predictably larger than life. They became gaudy and overstated. Lyndon developed into a towering and intimidating Texas blowhard, who bullied his way into the private reserves of the upper crust because no one had the guts to throw him out. Too many of his "betters" were afraid of his backers and his power to risk snubbing him.

Likewise, Billy's combination of good works, good looks, and good image in the media, plus his army of devoted followers, gave him the power to walk through doors normally closed to upstart country boys. He had both Jesus and PR power on his side.

Like all prominent and influential men, Billy and Lyndon acquired certain hangups and personality blocks, along with their notoriety and power. In this regard they differ, but only in degree.

Johnson was plagued by a temper that drove him to the point of eye-for-eye vengeance. That was what blinded him into ultimate political downfall when the National Liberation Front of South Vietnam and the North Vietnamese defied him on the battlefield and refused to back down. He took it all as a personal affront, and he hit back harder, trying to achieve a victory he could not win. This emotional overreaction led to a personal and national failure of tragic proportions.

Billy, too had (and has) a temper almost as large as the size of his carefully nurtured public image of goodness. But unlike his Texas sidekick, Billy has managed to keep it out of sight, locked away behind the security fences of the Graham estate at Montreat. When he's angered by someone or something, he storms behind his modern-day moat, to fume and brood while his press aides keep outsiders skillfully at bay.

It is said that Billy never forgets or forgives an

enemy and that his fits of unseen rage have come more often since the downfall of Lyndon Johnson and, more recently, Richard Nixon. He keeps mental lists of critics, antiwar activists, and antiestablishment journalists, hoping to settle the score someday.

But that is only the overview of the Graham-Johnson relationship. The details of what went on between the two men provide a much more interesting and colorful scenario of American politics at work, a scenario that began in earnest on November 22, 1963, in Dallas, when a visibly shaken Lyndon Johnson took the oath of office aboard Air Force One.

Although Johnson had always coveted the presidency, Kennedy's sudden death caught LBJ painfully and frightfully ill-prepared. For one of the very few times in his life, Johnson found himself totally reliant on the judgment and advice of his friends, and his political enemies, as well.

On the friendly side of the ledger, he found Billy Graham, and he turned to the preacher even before Kennedy's body had been returned to Washington.

Billy urged Lyndon to see the difficult transition through and to take great care to stay on the good side of the Camelot people by keeping the Kennedy programs publicly intact for a reasonable period of mourning. Although Billy was flirting with his own thoughts about the presidency, he advised Johnson that it might be smart to start working on an "All the Way with LBJ" campaign for 1964. Lyndon wholeheartedly agreed.

By the summer of 1964, Johnson was taking full advantage of Graham's politically astute counseling, and Billy was out of the running and 100 percent back into LBJ's presidential corner, allowing his almost constant presence to serve as an unofficial endorsement.

It was hectic at the Democratic convention and

Lyndon Johnson had a bad case of convention-eve jit-
ters. There was talk that Bobby Kennedy and his
mother, Rose, might walk into the middle of the fray
and, despite the odds against them, try to steal the nomination. Short of that, they might sway the delegates
away from the Johnson machine, just enough to give the
nod to some dark horse.

It was a rough moment for the Texan, but Billy
Graham was right there in the Johnson suite to offer
strength. Billy assured Lyndon that Bobby Kennedy
was the man to beat when the big showdown vote
came. Billy truly believed that Kennedy was the man to
beat. If he hadn't felt that way, chances are he would
have been sipping Kennedy-imported Scotch with different people in a different hotel room on convention
eve.

As things turned out, Billy faith in Lyndon's delegates strength was well founded. Despite the specter of
Rose and Bobby, the 1964 convention went by the numbers all carefully dictated by the man in the White
House.

The convention began its four-day stand on
Monday, August 24, in that crumbling, seaside monument to hard times and Miss American beauty, Atlantic
City, New Jersey. Delegates and the media complained
about the tacky surroundings, even though an ample
supply of callgirls and hookers had been shipped in
from New York and other Eastern cities to accommodate
nonpartisan needs.

In spite of all of the press, television, and radio
coverage, the convention was windy and unspectacular.
Democratic National Chairman John Bailey had put
together a program based more on high-toned rhetoric
than on substantial or thought-provoking issues. The

White House had given Bailey the guidelines, and he had followed them to the largely meaningless letter.

The keynote address was delivered by Rhode Island Senate John Pastore. His usual eloquence and fire somehow got left back in Washington, as he plodded through the old, predictable lines about "recognizing responsibilities at home and abroad" . . . "providing strong and honest leadership" . . . "and meeting the challenge of the future." It was standard, village-square rally stuff: safe, self-serving, and uninspired.

By the second day of the convention, word swept across the floor that the Kennedy bid for a takeover didn't have enough key support. The delegates grew restive and anxious to get Johnson and Humphrey nominated so they could go home—especially when the gavel was turned over to the sleepy, senile hands of ancient House Speaker John McCormack. Under his confused, three-day reign as convention chairman, the delegates and the nation nearly nodded off to sleep. The platform was hashed out to conform with Johnson's "Great Society," and the yawns stretched from coast-to-coast.

The only remote sparks of life came during the nominations. Texas' John Connally kept his pre-Republican career alive, blustering above the bunting in behalf of his old friend Lyndon. In turn, California Governor Pat Brown used every superlative in his ample book to extol the virtues of Hubert Horatio Humphrey. It was more than a vice-presidential nominating speech: it was Brown's fully televised payment for Humphrey's help in the campaign against Richard Nixon in the 1962 governor's race. Hubert had done well by Pat, and Pat never forgot a favor.

Intermixed with all the fine words about the frontrunners, the convention agenda makers did their best

183

to entertain themselves and the nation with an old Democratic ploy—tearjerking. There were tributes to the life, times, and image of Jack Kennedy. Eleanor Roosevelt got her customary recognition. And even brutish, arm-twisting Sam Rayburn was remembered fondly by the party faithful whether they had liked Rayburn or not. After all, this was a Texas convention, controlled by Texans, for the greater glory of the biggest Texan of them all.

Of course, by the end of convention week, Lyndon Johnson had won the Democratic nomination. The Kennedys were clearly out for another four years, and Billy Graham was clearly in, even more than he had been before. The election came and went, the Republicans headed for the bunkers to hide and reorganize along more moderate lines, and Lyndon revamped FDR's New Deal into a contemporary Great Society.

1965 was a busy year for Billy along the crusading rail, with major revivals at home and abroad. But of all the crusades that year, the one in Houston was by far the most important, because it gave Johnson a well-publicized way to repay all that Graham loyalty and to make a few personal headlines in the bargain. In November 1965, President and Mrs. Johnson sat among sixty thousand people in the Houston Astrodome to see and hear Billy Graham preach the Gospel.

LBJ and Lady Bird had been to other crusades at other times, but never in the happy role of the nation's first couple. This time it was an absolute sensation as the Johnsons waved and smiled their way into the dome and down to the special presidential box, surrounded by secret-service men and an entourage of local Texas politicians hoping to share the glow of carefully aimed spotlights.

184

Lyndon was playing to a hometown audience and a guaranteed standing ovation with nationwide implications. Those who were there say the cheers and cowboy yells couldn't have been louder if the Houston Astros had finally climbed out of the second division to win the American League pennant.

All Billy Graham crusades are well orchestrated by his hand-picked staff of advance men and staging experts. But the Houston crusade was an absolute masterpiece of theatrics, with Billy and the president sharing top billing.

The man on the podium acknowledged the man in the box seat, and the favor was returned with equal flair while the galleries went berserk with awestricken applause.

Billy offered a prayer for Lyndon's continued reign, and sixty thousand voices roared forth the "amen." Even the sermon of the night was appropriately changed from its normal topic, to suit the needs and the image of the guest of honor. For a full forty minutes, Billy lectured the masses on the difficult job of being president in sinful times and how God somehow had cast his ballot for Lyndon Baines Johnson. It was a sermon that would have been laughed off the dais in Washington, but in less sophisticated Houston it produced the desired results. With the help of God and his good friend Billy Graham, the President kept his grass roots watered. A few years later, when LBJ found himself in the midst of a personal political drought, he would need all the Texas turf he could hang on to.

For all its obvious cornball dramatics, the Houston revival played well enough in the Eastern press—perhaps because the fourth estate had not yet lost faith in "country" exuberance and in Lyndon Johnson.

Even Washington columnist Marianne Means saw something warm and wonderful in the Johnson-Graham relationship when she sat down and typed:

> *It is understandable that they should get along so well. For there is a great deal of preacher in Lyndon Johnson and a great deal of politician in Billy Graham. Each, in his own way, is a dedicated but utterly realistic man. They are both products of the Southern Bible Belt; they share a fervent, homespun eloquence which has enabled them to stir the emotions of other men and rise to the peak of their professions.*

Although it was a bit starry-eyed, the Means' column did touch on the basic affinity the president and the preacher had for each other. But it says nothing about Johnson's need to be associated in public with "clean" image makers. Nor does it mention the fact that true believers in Texas—Johnson's "little people"—have given millions of dollars in donations to further Billy Graham's work.

1965 provided much more than a standing-room-only crowd in Houston. It also marked the beginning of almost nonstop informal contact between the two men. Billy and Ruth almost became members of the Johnson household, whether it was holding sway in the White House or cooking barbecue on the Texas ranch. Billy became every inch a key advisor to the president, openly relishing the importance it brought him.

In an interview with Edward Fiske, Billy took pride in having been there when Johnson found himself backed into tight corners by the likes of Billie Sol Estes and Walter Jenkins. In those days, no swindle or sex scandal was too big to keep the preacher from rallying behind the president and his reputation.

Billy told interviewer Fiske that it was simply an act of devotion to an uncommonly decent though misunderstood man:

> *I love to be around him because I love Texas, and he's all Texas. And I think you have to be in that Pedernales Valley to understand President Johnson. I understand a bit of the background of where he came from and what his roots were and what made him tick. And the things people thought of as crude were not crude to me, because I had been there and I knew what part of Texas he came from.*

That was a familiar theme for Billy in the 1960s and remains so even today when someone suggests that Lyndon Johnson was less than a saint. Billy insists that beneath his rough exterior and killer reputation, LBJ was a simple, good-natured man with a complete and well-used set of humanitarian instincts, which were reflected best of all in his domestic policies.

Johnson, seen through Billy's eyes, was a good, self-established Christian who patiently suffered slings and arrows from envious and evil detractors, while trying to cope with the most difficult job in the world. And when all else failed, says Billy, LBJ turned to his God for strength and guidance to see the struggle through.

That may have sounded good in 1965, but by 1968 even the Almighty couldn't help President Johnson pull himself from the morass in southeast Asia. The war in Vietnam was not going well, despite a quantum leap in American combat involvement. Johnson was assailed on one side by powerful factions that wanted a clear-cut victory and, on the other, by a fast-growing popular movement to give up and pull out.

Johnson stood by his guns, saying that the United States had a moral obligation to support South Vietnam until the battle was won on the side of democracy and an honorable peace. And Billy Graham dutifully carried that high-toned, head-in-the-sand philosophy with him on the crusade circuit. The president called for more time and more patience, and Billy called for the critics to be shut up. The pleas were eloquent and backed by plenty of appropriate scripture, but by the time 1968 arrived, they went largely unheeded, particularly in the increasingly rebellious Democratic-party ranks.

The primaries that year were a disaster for LBJ as the Kennedy specter rose again in the person of young Bobby. The party was splitting in half with the prospect of breaking apart completely. The end was very near.

Finally, the reality of defeat had to be faced. Billy sat within the inner circle at the White House on an evening in March 1968 and listened with disappointment, but no argument. The president told Billy and the others he would go nationwide on television to call for peacemaking in Asia, and to step out of the race for reelection.

Lyndon Johnson was at the lowest ebb of his long political career, surrounded by the men who shared the downfall with him. All, that is, save one—Billy Graham commiserated with Johnson's fall from grace, but he did not have to share it. Thanks to the assassination of Robert Kennedy and the day-late, dollar-short campaign of Hubert Humphrey, a Republican victory was in the wind.

And Billy smelled it just as clearly as the rest of the nation. His old friend Richard Nixon had returned from exile with enough conservative issues and enough money from the Vietnam hawks to make a strong bid for the ultimate office. The pollsters agreed that Nixon would just squeak by Hubert in November. The point spread was going to be slim, but Billy Graham was more than willing to gamble this time and go for broke on the odds.

The Quaker Monarchy

Most political experts now agree that if Hubert Humphrey had been given just two or three more weeks of campaigning time, Billy Graham would have lost his bet on Richard Nixon. But the election laws and luck were on Dick Nixon's side in 1968, with Billy Graham's vocal and thankful blessing.

Nixon's return to power provided Billy with one of his most impressive and talked-about moments of glory —a tour de force unmatched by any White House visitor in history. He stayed on the premises while one president packed up and left and a new one rolled through the front gates to move in.

On the very weekend before Nixon's inauguration, in January 1969, Billy and Ruth were called to the White House for a last long visit with the Johnson clan. In those final hours of power, Johnson was in the depths of depression—some say bitter to the point of angry shouts and sudden crying jags.

Locked away in the presidential study, the ousted chief executive and his favorite preacher sat up late, talking about what had gone wrong and what lay ahead.

Certainly, Johnson was nicely fixed for life back on the Texas Ranch, but he looked and acted like a man on the verge of bankruptcy. What he valued most was the power of his lost presidency, and the power would soon pass out of his hands, to one of his oldest and least-respected enemies. By cruel fate and default, Nixon was a personal tragedy to the inconsolable LBJ.

189

Billy, of course, was properly sympathetic with Johnson's agony, but stood up against his old Texas friend in defense of Richard Nixon. In one of their few known disagreements, Billy argued long and loud that Nixon was a far better man to fill the large Johnsonian shoes than the likes of Hubert Humphrey or, much worse, another Kennedy.

As if to prove his loyalty to both men, Billy stayed next to Johnson until the very end on the inaugural platform, then promptly stepped forward to the podium to deliver a prayer for Nixon's success as the new president. To outsiders, it appeared a blatant contradiction of friendships. But to Billy—and to the realistic Johnson —it was nothing more and nothing less than good politics.

For the first time since he had begun hanging around the White House, Graham had managed to survive a change of power without getting tossed out on the street and having to fight his way back in again. The Graham incumbency had been a startling success, but it had not come overnight. In truth, it had been in the making since 1948 and 1949, when the Hearst papers saved Billy from oblivion in Los Angeles.

Billy's longstanding relationship with Nixon began in a back-handed way even before he had ever laid eyes on the future president. Nixon's ardent Quaker parents were regular and devoted visitors to Billy's tent-show revivals and often chatted with him about the joy their son had brought to them by committing himself to Christ as a teenager. The evangelist told them he shared in their joy and prayed that their son would succeed in the halls of Congress. The prayer was answered.

Not until May 1950 did Nixon and Graham finally cross paths and begin walking hand in hand down the same road to the 1968 victory. As the legend goes, Billy was sitting in the senate dining room, sharing conversation and bean soup with Senator Clyde Hoey of North Carolina. When Nixon passed by the table to answer a phone call from his office, Hoey flagged him down for an introduction to his smiling young constituent.

It must have been love at first sight, because Nixon returned to the table to talk at length and did not leave until he got Billy to join him for a round of golf at Burning Tree Country Club, that very afternoon. The score is not recorded, but Billy and Dick became a permanent twosome, on and off the links.

The early fifties were a time of unprecedented stress in the American experience. Truman had grown unpopular as the head of both his party and the nation. A war that almost no one understood raged, then bogged down, in faraway Korea. Worse, the victories over Germany and Japan just a few years earlier had been tarnished by the spread of Communist influence around the globe.

The time was ripe for Americans to go on another postwar Red hunt, and much of the nation eagerly beat the bushes under the frightening and demagogic leadership of Senator Joe McCarthy. As the cold war grew colder, McCarthy's appeal grew warmer to a country-wide constituency of people who were too frightened and too frustrated to see the sham of their new messiah.

In those early days of the mid-century decade, Richard Nixon was at the forefront, right along with McCarthy, in the search for Communists within the government. While McCarthy slugged away at the nonexistent threat, Nixon stood close by, holding his coat. He got himself a reputation for being a tough, uncompromising foe of Communism and, in turn, won himself a vice-presidential nomination in 1952. The GOP accurately sensed that Americans would feel a lot safer if Ike had a resident hatchet man on twenty-four-hour call.

Billy Graham, of course, was ecstatic over Nixon's good fortune at the 1952 convention. In those days, Billy was decidedly more fundamentalist, and he had openly supported both Nixon and McCarthy in their fight against godless Communism. Although he did not offer public endorsements of the Eisenhower-Nixon ticket, he did utter prayers that "American voters would select men with the vision and Christian will to stand up and turn aside the unholy threat from behind the Iron Curtain."

Following the one-sided Eisenhower victory, the Nixon-Graham relationship grew steadily closer until it became an intimate alliance that served both men well in public and private. Dick made sure that Billy met the right people in the right places; and Billy returned the favor by boosting his often-criticized friend as "a good and decent man" and a "true God-fearing American."

To cement the relationship beyond anyone's doubt, Nixon paid Billy the supreme compliment by bringing wife Pat to Yankee Stadium for a personal appearance at the crucial Graham 1957 New York crusade. The vice-president had come as Dwight Eisenhower's personal representative but wound up standing before the fifty-thousand-plus audience to speak for himself. He praised the man standing next to him as "one of the greatest men alive in the world today." Billy said thank you with one of his very best "God protect Dick" prayers.

Of course, a public friendship like that has its drawbacks, as Billy quickly discovered when it came time for Ike to step down and for Dick Nixon to step forward.

Even Graham admits that he was suddenly under

pressure to come forth and declare his unqualified support for Nixon's 1960 campaign. The squeeze came from the very men Nixon had introduced him to during the eight Eisenhower years, and Billy was clearly on the spot. He wanted to keep his options open with the Kennedys, just in case, but, on the other hand, he couldn't risk alienating the big-money men who ran the Republican party.

Rather than wrestle with the decision alone, Billy turned to the one man who could let him have his cake and eat it too—Nixon. The two men met, in Washington, and after two hours they emerged with Billy's problem solved quite nicely. Nixon had decided Billy could avoid committing himself by staying out of the campaign.

In return for that free pass, Billy went crusading overseas during the 1960 Nixon-Kennedy campaign. The thankful evangelist deliberately put himself beyond the reach of American reporters and political opportunists, skillfully using his ministry as a cover until the storm blew over. In the end, Billy managed to survive the gale; Nixon did not. He lost to Kennedy by an eyelash.

During the next seven years, private citizen Nixon stayed out of the national limelight, but he worked hard on the small-time level, campaigning on behalf of every Republican office seeker he could lay his endorsement on. He was an eager volunteer to help raise GOP funds in tank towns from coast to coast.

Nixon shook local hands by the thousands and pounded down lukewarm chicken à la king by the ton, hoping to build up enough grass-roots debts to maneuver his way back into position for another shot at the presidency. It was hard and sometimes humiliating work for a man like Nixon, but he knew it had to be done. After his ballot-box disasters in 1960 and 1962, no one was going to do it for him.

While Nixon fought for a new footing Billy Graham did quite nicely. He weathered the lean days of the Kennedy administration, to find favor with Lyndon Johnson. But despite his good fortune, Billy was every inch the good Samaritan in Richard Nixon's out-of-office life, always on hand to offer moral and spiritual support when Dick began brooding about his bad luck. The two spent time together every time their paths crossed, whether it was duffing around a golf course or enjoying *nouveau-riche* opulence aboard the Key Biscayne yacht of millionaire Florida businessman Bebe Rebozo.

By 1967, a ray of light poked through into Nixon's long, dark tunnel. It became clear to careful observers that Johnson was in serious trouble over the Vietnam issue—trouble serious enough perhaps, to cut him down to size in the 1968 election. It was equally apparent that the Republican party could not repeat the right-wing mistake of another Barry Goldwater.

That's when Nixon's loyal party work began to pay off. GOP strategists were looking for a slightly more moderate candidate who could appeal to both the big-money hawks in the East and the millions of war-weary but confused voters in Middle America. Nixon was slick enough to fill the contradictory bill, if only the party could figure out some way to erase his "loser" image and make him an acceptable package for sale in the predominantly rural South.

Hoping to kill those two birds with one stone, they turned again to Billy Graham and pressured him to get involved and endorse Nixon for president.

Suddenly, it was 1960 all over again. Billy found himself caught between his friendship for Nixon (*and* Johnson!) and his instinctive reluctance to take a firm political stand that might prove embarrassing if he wound up publicly supporting a loser.

Even when Johnson dropped out of the race, Billy went to Nixon and his advisors to plead for another grant of neutrality. They let the worried preacher dangle helplessly at the end of their string until a compromise, of sorts, was worked out by a Nixon aide named Harry S. Dent.

Dent was in charge of the Nixon campaign in the South, and the Graham compromise was part and parcel of the overall Southern invasion plan. Under the terms Billy agreed to, he was to remain technically silent about the candidate of his choice until the very last days of the campaign. In return for being allowed to stay off the record that long, Billy was expected to work unofficially toward delivering Dixie into Nixon's hands.

Figuring he had made the best possible deal under the circumstances, Billy came through with flying colors. He promoted Nixon behind closed doors with Southern business- and clergymen. He took an active part in a series of televised question-and-answer programs, paid for and produced by the Nixon for President Campaign. Overall, he did everything short of standing up before the nation and screaming, "Nixon's the One!" with his arms around the Statue of Liberty and Uncle Sam.

Finally, just one week before election day, Billy made completely good on his promise to Harry Dent, with the ultimate Graham-plan ploy. Word leaked out that Billy had cast an absentee ballot for Richard M. Nixon and his unknown running mate, Spiro T. Agnew.

The press, needless to say, smelled a rat. But Harry Dent played the innocent, though lucky, bystander when reporters asked him if the leak was a political setup. It was nothing of the sort, he protested; it was just one of those fortunate but unplanned breaks of the political game. But, no sooner had he proclaimed his noncomplicity in the affair, than Dent flooded the country with pro-Nixon propaganda built neatly around Billy's "surprise" absentee-ballot endorsement.

As Harry put it after the election, "That [ballot] was all I needed. I used it in all our TV commercials, right down to the end!"

Harry was being less than candid again. He failed to mention that the ads had been put into production a full three to four weeks before Billy even picked up his pencil to vote for the Nixon-Agnew ticket.

Nor did Dent and his fellow campaign plotters talk much about a secret meeting held months before the election, on the very night Nixon got the nomination from the Republican convention. The topic of discussion was critical for ultimate success in November: who would be the best candidate for vice-president? The outcome of the meeting became apparent the very next day, when Agnew got the nod with a unanimous floor vote. But the details of the late-night session that got Spiro the job did not emerge until much later, after Nixon was safely elected to office.

By Billy's own account, he stopped by the Nixon suite at the Shoreham to congratulate his old friend on winning the nomination. (In truth, Billy had been summoned to the inner sanctum by Nixon, at the urging of Harry Dent.)

In addition to a few GOP financial backers, Billy found the room filled with top party leaders giving their opinions. Barry Goldwater was there, wide-eyed and pressing hard to make Ronald Reagan the vice-presidential nominee. The dictatorial Senator Strom Thurmond argued long and loudly for his man, Agnew. Even

Thomas Dewey was allowed to sit in with his two cents' worth.

Each man in the room was allowed to express his views while a shirt-sleeved Nixon played the role of ring master and, on several occasions, mediator when fights broke out. When Billy's turn to speak came up, the collective groans could be heard all the way out in the hall. He told the group he thought Senator Mark Hatfield would make a good vice-president.

Billy later wrote: "I said, 'I think I would prefer Mark Hatfield. First of all, he's a great Christian leader. He's almost a clergyman. He's been an educator, and he's taken a more liberal stand on most issues than you, and I think that the ticket needs that kind of balance.'"

Billy's Christian heart was in the right place, but his political head certainly was not. Mark Hatfield couldn't have been a poorer choice, and everyone in the room except Billy knew it. Placing Nixon next to Hatfield on the convention podium would have made the presidential candidate look like Attila the Hun by comparison.

Even more important, Hatfield was decidedly on the side of the Arab cause in the Middle East. That ran sharply across the grain of the Nixon pro-Israeli policy and would have seriously hampered efforts to tap campaign money from Tel Aviv's many rich and influential American friends.

Thus, Billy's man was rejected, along with most of the others, until the choice boiled down to just two names—Agnew and Reagan. The participants in the meeting took their favorite sides and battled it out until 5:00 A.M., when Nixon cast the final and deciding vote in favor of the Greek-American miniconservative from Maryland.

As the long meeting broke up and everyone stumbled off for a few hours of sleep, Billy paused at the door and shook Nixon's hand, assuring his friend that Agnew was the best man after all. "I saw him as a man of honesty and genuine integrity," Billy admitted later.

During the campaign of 1968, Billy spent more time crisscrossing the land than even Nixon did. Mixing the salvation business with favor paying, Billy had a good word for the Republican candidate at every stop. For good measure, Billy invited the Nixons to drop in on his crusade in Pittsburgh for a little bit of deeply moving television coverage.

On September 11, 1968, the Nixons took Billy up on his offer and sauntered into the revival, waving and flashing victory signs to the other penitents in the arena. The Reverend welcomed them with outstretched arms, beckoning them to come forth where the cameras could pick them up a bit better.

And come forth they did, to sit and listen to Billy deliver an awe-inspiring campaign pitch. He looked heavenward into the middle-class section of the audience and spoke warmly, describing his friendship with Dick as "one of the most cherished I have had with anyone!" The crowd cheered, and Billy came right back with a human touch that brought mist to his eyes, praising his celebrated guest for his "generosity, tremendous constraint of temper, and his integrity in totaling his golf score!" The crowd roared with laughter and approval.

At the end of his remarks Graham gripped the edges of the podium, arms locked straight, and silently stared at the multitude. It was time for the big finish. The evangelist pulled himself fully erect and asked the crowd to forget party affiliation and "pray for Richard Nixon *and* America!"

The evening was a fabulous success for the Nixon

cause, a spiritual and political love feast that generated miles of wire-service copy for the news outlets of the nation. The candidate walked out of the Pittsburgh rally surrounded by a halo and the media. He told reporters, "This was one of the most moving religious experiences of my life."

And so it went, as September slipped by and the campaign headed into October and the home stretch. Billy stuck to his promise to defend the Nixon honor every time it was attacked within his hearing.

On October 16, Billy lashed out at the Under Secretary of State George Ball, after that diplomat had raised some personal questions about the candidate's basic honesty. In a statement issued from his Minneapolis headquarters, an angry Graham told the world that Nixon was one of the most honest men in politics: "I can testify that he is a man of high moral principles. And while I do not intend to publicly endorse any political candidate, as some clergymen are doing, I maintain the right to help put the record straight when a friend is smeared." Billy exercised that right even after all the votes were counted and his man was proclaimed president.

Nixon carried the South and Middle America as planned, with a high voter turnout from the teeming masses of confirmed Graham believers. And though the victory was merely the result of plain old-fashioned backroom American politicking, Billy gave a lot of the credit to God's good graces.

The preacher went nationwide on CBS radio's "World of Religion" program immediately after the election to predict ecumenically that "Nixon's deep religious roots will be a factor, as in the Kennedy administration and that of Eisenhower and that of Johnson."

After covering those important spiritual bases,

Billy went on to tell the radio audience the time had come to quit picking on Nixon's shady background:

"He has a great sense of moral integrity. I think he will become a respected president because I think he will come across to the American people.

"I have never seen any indication of, or agreed with, the label that his enemies have given him of 'Tricky Dick.' In the years I've known him, he's never given any indication of being tricky."

Nixon's election instantly elevated Billy Graham to the de facto cabinet-level status of unofficial White House chaplain, just as Eisenhower's had sixteen years earlier. But this time around, the job carried more responsibilities and many more opportunities because Billy was personally closer to Nixon than he had been to Ike, or even Johnson, for that matter.

Time magazine portrayed the president and his preacher as brothers under the philosophical and political skin. Both, said *Time*, enjoyed large, Middle-Amer. can constituencies and shared identical views on the major issues: issues like crime in the streets, black militancy and the antiwar protests.

Quoting the *Time* article: "like Nixon, Graham considers the Supreme Court has 'gone too far' in favoring criminals. He supports Black Power but only if it means 'a feeling of self-respect,' not violence or civil disobedience.

"He believes that the demonstrators at the Democratic Convention in Chicago were 'wonderful kids, idealists . . . but manipulated by a small, well-organized core that wanted confrontation.' The Chicago police overreacted, but 'I don't know how some of the policemen restrained themselves that long.'"

From the very beginning of the Nixon reign, Billy served as the president's preachmaster general, to be trotted out at appropriate times to underscore the White House link with God and his goodness. A check of the busy Graham appointment book clearly reveals that Billy gave Nixon's needs top priority.

For example, during September 1969, nine months into the new administration, Billy flew to the Pacific coast three times to help the president at well-covered public events.

The first time, Billy was one of two clergymen to sit down and break bread with Nixon and the *Apollo XI* moon-walk astronauts, Armstrong, Aldrin, and Collins. Billy delivered a short prayer, thanking the Great Mission Controller in the Sky for the trio's safe return, and Nixon took the credit for the space program, even though Kennedy and Johnson had done most of the work.

Graham's second September sojourn was equally important to enchancing the Nixon image, although it was less festive and more businesslike. With attaché case in hand, the preacher sat down with the president's hand-picked people for a board meeting of the Richard Nixon Foundation. Like most foundations, the RNF was dedicated to high-flown humanitarian pursuits, not to mention glorifying the man after whom it was named.

Billy's third Western visit was a whirlwind of fun and games. He played conspicuous tagalong with Nixon as they took a ride on Air Force One. He took part in a ceremony honoring Lady Bird Johnson and played a total of three rounds of golf in the warm California sun. It was a hectic few days, topped off by a party around the pool at San Clemente—an excellent way to combine the good life with some good press coverage.

When the Dick and Billy Show wasn't on the road it played to standing room at the White House. No matter how busy the presidential calendar may have been, Billy could walk in unannounced, to visit the boss. And unlike most, Billy could always pick up a telephone and get right through to the Oval Office. There are stories, still told by former White House aides, of how Nixon kept heavyweights like Henry Kissinger and Senator Mike Mansfield on hold, while he small-talked long distance with the man on the hill in North Carolina.

Of course, the close relationship between the two men was more than just mutual love and respect. The Nixon "buddy system" played an important part in the White House plan to keep the "Silent Majority" reminded and reassured of Richard's basic goodness and honesty. Some people put pictures of Jesus in their offices to achieve the same effect, but Nixon went one step better by carrying a living, breathing saint with him wherever he went. Billy Graham was always close to Nixon's right hand, and the president did everything possible to remind the public of it.

There was a backlash effect, but luckily for Nixon, it was confined to a small segment of what he considered professional cynics and critics. They were the same journalists, politicians, and private citizens whom Vice-President Agnew called "nabobs of negativism." Privately, the president sloughed them off angrily as "sons of bitches."

Writers like Gary Wills called the Graham-Nixon friendship and the administration that exploited it an alliance of moral dwarfs. Will Campbell, a high-ranking Baptist minister, accused Billy of selling out the Gospel to become, "a false court prophet who tells Nixon and the Pentagon what they want to hear." And more than one news commentator took to the typewriter or microphone to suggest that Billy was just too dazzled by his White House status to realize he was being used to make a bad man look good.

Billy hated the attacks as much as Nixon did, but neither of them seemed upset enough to back off on their constant companionship. By 1970, Billy had become a conduit for administration propaganda, and the Graham organization had been converted into a far-reaching forum for the president to use whenever he saw fit.

There is no better example of that than the Knoxville Billy Graham Rally on Thursday, May 28, 1970, in the sixty-thousand-seat Volunteer Stadium, on the University of Tennessee campus. The crusade was another in a long series of university tent shows designed to bring more young people into the Graham fold and offset the decline of older converts and donors as they died off. On the surface, it looked like God's business as usual.

But on the seventh day of the crusade for youth, Richard Nixon stepped in to alter the goals a bit. He arrived at Volunteer Stadium to defend his record in office—and it needed considerable defending, because Nixon had just expanded the war by sending American troops into Cambodia.

Actually, Nixon's Knoxville appearance was anything but a last-minute affair. It was a carefully calculated effort by both the White House and the BGEA to combat all the bad press stirred by the Cambodian incursion. The University of Tennessee was selected as the target campus for one reason: It was a conservative, fraternity- and football-oriented school where Nixon could say what he wanted to say, with minimum threat of getting run off the campus. It was a pro-Nixon School, not Kent State.

Picking the place for Nixon to defend his honor was simple, compared to the elaborate shell game that had to be played out before the president could even set foot on campus. The first order of business was to get the Graham crusade into Volunteer Stadium, so Nixon could move in and use it.

That job fell to Ralph Frost, the man in charge of booking concerts and other entertainment for student and faculty functions at the University of Tennessee. The Nixon-Graham advance men contacted him early and asked him to get the arrangements rolling. In dutiful response, Frost gathered a petition asking the University to welcome and co-sponsor the crusade. The petition was doomed to failure from the start, because university policy banned any such close association with any religious function. Frost knew that, but he was merely going through the motions, to get the school clearly on record as a disinterested party.

The next step followed directly from the first. With the university off the hook, Frost left campus and asked a group of leading Knoxville Baptists and businessmen if they would like to sponsor Billy's revival. To no one's surprise, they were delighted to assume the task. They marched with Frost right back to the campus to rent Volunteer Stadium for a ten-day stand.

The university's president, Andy Holt, only too glad to go along with the deal, instructed his Knoxville chancellor, Charles Weaver, to turn the stadium over to Graham for a token rental of two thousand dollars a day —a modest twenty thousand for the entire run of the revival. Holt's cooperation in the arrangements had been guaranteed from the start: He was a close friend of Billy's, he had signed the original Frost petition; and he had even accepted a warm invitation to attend the rallies and take an active part at the speakers' podium. (In fact, Holt delivered a plea for donations at the first rally.) Holt was the joker in a stacked deck. It was up to him to make sure the other cards fell into place, to clear the way for Billy's campus beachhead and Nixon's final invasion.

Holt huddled with Knoxville city fathers to make sure appearances were kept and all plans carried out. Civic and business organizations and a full list of local churches were cajoled into endorsing the crusade. Extra buses were rerouted past the stadium to handle pilgrims, and police duty assignments were changed to keep traffic and potential protesters moving in the right direction.

Police involvement was essential to Holt, because a nasty rebellion was afoot in the land after Cambodia, and there was a chance of trouble when the president arrived on the scene. No one worried about the majority of kids on the University of Tennessee campus. They had voted overwhelmingly in favor of White House war policies in a special straw poll. But there was concern about the two hundred or so followers of a conservative student turned radical, by the name of Barry Bozeman. He was a resident pain in the neck to university officials, and he made it plain that he and his people were going to give the chief executive a vocal unwelcome reception.

Holt asked the Knoxville police to prepare for the worst, on the off chance that Bozeman and his dissenters might get a major protest rolling with the whole nation looking on. The local authorities took their assignment to heart and unearthed a little-used Tennessee statute (TCA 39-1204) that made it a crime to disrupt a religious service.

Under the law, the Knoxville police had the power to arrest any long-hair in sight for simply opening his mouth anywhere near the stadium. What was more, the cops could confiscate and destroy banners and placards on the spot, no matter what the U.S. Constitution had to say about free speech and the right to assembly. The White House, Billy Graham, and Andy Holt couldn't have asked for a more timely and helpful law, even if they had sat down to write it themselves.

Nixon waited in Washington while Billy got the Knoxville crusade off to a rousing and peaceful start. By the time the president's big night arrived, it looked as if the plan couldn't possibly fail. But fail it did, the very second the Presidential limousine roared into view under motorcycle escort. Bozeman's radical raiders were waiting for Nixon at the very gates of triumph. The dissenters numbered about one thousand, thanks to a last-minute alliance with antiwar faculty members and itinerant protesters from distant campuses.

The president was visibly upset by the familiar chants of "Bullshit! Bullshit! Bullshit!" and "Stop the crap and end the war!" This was not the reception his staffers had promised, and Nixon was obviously angry, despite his forced smiles and frantic, flailing victory signs.

The secret service wasn't any more pleased with the welcome than their boss was, and the order was issued to "make those bastards shut up and keep their distance." The Knoxville police responded by calling for backup units, which only made the situation meaner and more potentially explosive.

Nixon and his party got inside the stadium without incident but soon found out that Bozeman and his noisy followers had outplanned Andy Holt again. Hecklers were scattered all over the stands, carefully intermixed with the pro-Nixon forces. The dissidents had counted on a red-neck reaction, and they got it. Every time a protester shouted an insult toward the stage, a thousand angry nonprotesters would shout back, until even Billy's booming baritone couldn't be heard over the din.

The tribute to the president was turned into a shambles, but Nixon couldn't back down, even though Billy reportedly gave him the opportunity to do so.

Bracing himself against the boos and catcalls, the President rose to his feet, clutched his notes to his chest, and sprinted to center stage with execution-day bravado. He talked about the war as if it were an abstract football game. "Even if we are on the twenty-yard line," he proclaimed, "we are going to be over that goal line before we are through!" The anti-Nixon people howled at the tacky metaphor, and the pro-Nixonians howled back at the howling, forcing Nixon to stop and raise his arms for quiet like a football quarterback trying to hear his own signals.

Billy could be seen scowling toward Andy Holt as Nixon plunged ahead, trying to get control of his own supporters long enough to get the speech over and done with. The old campaigner tried every trick in his well-worn book, but the crowd was having too good a time to stop and listen. Finally, Nixon gave up and cut short his prepared remarks with a sweaty smirk and the antiheckler line he always used when critics refused to be cowed into silence: "I'm just glad there seems to be a rather more solid majority on my side, than on the other side, tonight!"

End of speech. End of rally. End of the University of Tennessee as the ideal place for Richard Nixon to explain his ever-expanding war.

There was a touch of electronic irony to the Knoxville debacle. Under Billy's personal direction, the entire night had been recorded by the crusade's closed-circuit television system, for distribution and playback on commercial stations all over the country. On videotape, Nixon came off looking like a winner instead of a loser. The microphones made the shouting match in the bleachers sound like cheers of encouragement for the chief executive. The dissenters never came into camera range, and it was impossible to detect that Mr. Nixon's hands were shaking, from the moment he opened his mouth till he headed for the exit. Thanks to luck and Billy's media knowhow, the evening had not been a total loss.

The city of Knoxville and the university were in dutch with the White House, and everyone knew it. But the police and politicians didn't dare settle their score with protesters until Billy packed up his tent and headed back to North Carolina, to hide and hate behind the walls of his fortress. With Billy gone from the scene, the Knoxville folks came down hard on Bozeman and the others.

Arrest teams swept across the campus picking up the students who had been photographed while raising hell on Nixon night. City patrol cars fanned out through the community, hitting every antiwar gathering place and every "hippie" commune listed on the police department subversive list. Two full-time faculty members were pulled in and booked for aiding and abetting the youthful wrongdoers. Even university records were used to track down students that the flying squads were unable to find on the street.

The frenzy of retribution lasted for the better part of a week, until eighty professors and instructors became outraged enough to meet and draw up a letter of protest to those responsible for the arrests. Even White House attorney Len Garment became frightened enough by the Gestapo tactics to fire off a telegram to the Knoxville mayor, saying that enough was enough. The mayor ignored Garment's appeal on the grounds that the law had to be upheld to discourage future un-American demonstrations.

In the end, the runaway overreaction was stopped by the very man who had helped create it, Andy Holt. Two hundred of his own students blackmailed him into calling off the dogs, by giving him a signed confession that they had heckled the president. Rather than turn them all in and face the possible wrath of the rest of the student body, Holt went running to Knoxville City Hall. Within an hour, the arrests came to a halt, ending what one deeply disturbed professor called "The Rape of the University of Tennessee."

If anything, the Knoxville crusade should have warned both Nixon and Billy Graham that their joint appearances were not doing a thing to bring the war-torn nation back together. But logic did not always prevail in those days of 1970 and the administration was hellbent to keep using Billy as long as it could help keep the president alive in middle-class, middle-income Middle America.

This was a classic case of misreading the mood of the nation, because even the Silent Majority was beginning to go sour on Vietnam— a fact of life that bloomed, full-flower, with Billy's second big mistake of the year: Honor America Day.

It was to be the Fourth of July celebration to end all Fourth of July celebrations, the alleged brainchild of Reader's Digest president Hobart Lewis. He wanted Americans of all political stripes to set aside their differences and flock to Washington to forgive and forget and watch history's biggest fireworks display.

Nixon was 100 percent in favor of Honor America Day, especially when his favorite preacher and his favorite comedian, Bob Hope, volunteered to help set it up. Hope would be in charge of the gala and patriotic entertainment. Billy would see to providing religious services and top-name clergymen to conduct them.

The result was predictable. Extremists from both sides of the war issue showed up to harass each other for the benefit of the TV cameras. It was the same old routine with the pot-smoking flag burners on the left, the Reverend Carl McIntire's Commie hunters on the right, and thousands of confused tourists and everyday people caught between the two.

The president was nowhere near the huge gathering. He was relaxing and watching it all on television at his San Clemente retreat, carefully avoiding the mistake of Knoxville. But even though Nixon was three thousand miles away from the action, his voice and his dogma poured forth from Billy Graham's mouth in what amounted to a long-distance Edgar Bergen and Charlie McCarthy act.

Billy stood sweating in front of the Lincoln Memorial as the sun beat down upon the restive throng. He gazed out over the multitude and delivered the Gospel according to St. Richard: Honor thy nation and its institutions; honor the brave Americans fighting for Democracy; close thy mouth in order that the nation's wounds may heal; and pray for the Republican administration, everlasting. Amen!

Honor America Day did little to bring opposing factions closer together, but nearly everyone agreed that the fireworks show was terrific.

Even though Nixon eventually had to pull out of Vietnam, his political career flourished. With Billy by his side the president crushed the fumbling George McGovern in the 1972 election. He glowed when the bewildered, half-starved POWs stepped out of brutal confinement into the glare and blare of brass-band receptions and television lights. And with Billy's best wishes he flew away to Peking to rub elbows with old enemies and tour the Great Wall. The reign of King

Richard and his preachmaster seemed assured until 1976. But in the midst of all the blatant self-aggrandizement and the joy of victory, Nixon's second-class Camelot came undone. The throne-room ceiling fell down on the monarch's head with a bang heard in every astounded capital of the world.

Watergate! The third-rate burglary of 1972 suddenly became the crime of the century. Men with unknown names like Dean, Butterfield, and Woodward and Bernstein suddenly became household words. There was talk of a criminal coverup, violated civil rights, Oval Office tape gaps, dirty tricks, paper shredders, and violent threats to life and limb.

Agnew was swept away for being a common crook, and there were persistent rumors that Nixon might join his closest aides in a federal-prison cell block. The bitter, unexpected end of Nixon's public life was very much in sight on the horizon.

With the president well on his way to impeachment, Graham found himself holding the bag on the question of his old friend's integrity. In the early days of the scandal, Billy had dismissed the charges as "unfounded and absurd." But now it was nitty-gritty time, and Billy did the only smart thing left open to him —he began to back down in his ardent defense of the president. In the January 4, 1974, issue of *Christianity Today*, Billy conceded that Nixon had made some errors in judgment about Watergate. And in trusting the likes of John Mitchell, H. R. Haldeman, and John Ehrlichman.

"I can make no excuses for Watergate," Billy lamented. "The actual break-in was a criminal act, and some of the things that surround Watergate, too, were not only unethical, but criminal. I condemn it and deplore it. It has hurt America."

But true to his friendship, Billy told *Christianity Today* that he wasn't about to walk into the White House like the biblical prophet Nathan and publicly censure Nixon for sinning. "As far as I know, the President has not been formally charged with a crime. Mistakes and blunders have been made. Some of them involved moral and ethical questions, but at this point, if I have anything to say to the President, it will be in private."

On several occasions the two men met and discussed the Watergate dilemma at great length, but what they said was never revealed. Billy emerged from the sessions critical of the president for making "mistakes" but still on his side as a friend.

The Graham loyalty to "Nixon the man" remained intact to almost the very end, even in late May 1974, when the White House begrudgingly released transcripts of the Watergate tapes, revealing that the president used a gutter vocabulary to conduct his business, legal and otherwise.

In a May 29 statement released at Montreat, Billy was careful to mix indignation with understanding. "I must confess this has been a profoundly disturbing and disappointing experience. One cannot but deplore the moral tone implied in these papers . . . and though we know that other Presidents have used equally objectionable language, it does not make it right."

Billy went on to express astonishment at Nixon's transformation, as reflected in the celebrated transcripts.

"What comes through in these tapes is not the man I have known for many years. Other mutual friends have made the same observation.

"But our repudiation of wrongdoing and our condemnation of evil must be tempered by compassion for the wrongdoers. Many a stone is being cast by persons whose own lives could not bear like scrutiny. Therefore, we dare not be self-righteous.

"The President is my friend and I have no intention of forsaking him now."

With that statement to his public, Billy Graham said no more about Watergate, until Nixon swallowed what was left of his pride and resigned.

The scandal left Nixon exiled with a mountain of debts and top billing in the American History Rogues Gallery. Billy, on the other hand, had been able to step neatly off the sinking ship, barely getting his socks wet. Billy survived the disaster with only a few bruises to his reputation.

In the three years since his ultimate humiliation, Nixon has brooded like a modern-day Napoleon on a West Coast Saint Helena. He has locked himself away from prying eyes, going through the motions of a pretend White House routine—even to the point of demanding that his aides address him as "Mr. President."

Each day he sits, dressed uncomfortably in a suit, laboring over his memoirs, calling old friends on the phone, and holding audience with approved visitors. Among them is Billy Graham, who still sees his old friend Dick whenever his ministry takes him within side-trip distance of San Clemente. Insiders say the relationship is still warm and intimate, even though the former president refuses to admit, much less repent, his sins. Billy, as always, understands and has mercy on Richard Nixon's soul.

It's the least the preachmaster general can do to say thanks for the days of glory Nixon shared with him

—especially when most of Nixon's oldest and biggest supporters still control the inner workings of the Republican party and may, one day, provide Billy Graham with another president to add to his collection.

The Fallow Ford Years

Perhaps the biggest single victim of the Nixon downfall was Gerald R. Ford, the man assigned the incredible task of trying to hold the nation together long enough for the election of an honest president.

At first blush, the president-by-default looked like the congressional "village idiot"—lovable but hopelessly ill-suited for any job bigger than house minority leader. When Ford got Nixon off the hook with a full pardon, the cry went up that the fix was in and that Gerry was another Watergate hack who had managed not to get caught. The media and the Democrats braced themselves for the worst but got a reasonably pleasant surprise instead.

Although Gerald Ford was not destined to become the twentieth-century version of Abe Lincoln, he was certainly not the much-feared instant replay of Richard Nixon. Ford and his staff made a determined effort to rid the White House of the dead remains of scandal. The pomp and circumstance of previous years was swept away. Along with it went Rebozo and the other charter members of the Nixon fan club.

Suddenly there was a new pecking order on the official presidential guest list, and Billy Graham found his name dangerously close to the bottom, just as it had been when Kennedy ran the show. Billy was a holdover from the Nixon entourage, and the Ford administration wanted him as far out of sight as possible without insulting every Bible-belt Baptist in the country.

This time, Billy took his medicine like a man—some say out of deference to Nixon. Billy sat down and knocked out a prayer for President Ford, published in the December 1974 issue of the *Ladies Home Journal*. After urging God to help get Ford through the next thirty months, Billy just couldn't resist one last plug, for old times' sake: "We pray especially for our former president and for his family at this time, that in the days ahead they may know the peace that only Thou canst give . . . just as he sought to bring peace to the world."

Whether Billy's prayer helped Richard Nixon much is debatable, but it certainly got results for President Ford. Despite his inability to get the economy under control, or to walk without bumping into things, the chief executive was able to keep the nation going and even win the nomination at the 1976 GOP convention. It was a credit to Ford's stamina and political know-how, acquired, in large part, from the wily Everett Dirksen.

Graham sat on his Carolina mountaintop, testing the political winds and reading the Gallup polls. A "born-again" Christian named Jimmy Carter was ahead of Ford in all the tallies, but the gap was narrowing fast as election day drew closer. Since Carter was not in need of salvation or a resident minister, and since Gerry seemed to have a chance to pull off a narrow victory, Billy decided to stick with the incumbent.

A week or so before the ballots were cast, Billy talked his way into the White House for one of his few brief visits with Ford and his advisers. Within minutes, he was back outside telling reporters that he thought Ford was a good president and that Jimmy Carter should have had better sense than to confess to "mental adultery" in *Playboy* magazine. It was hardly a wholehearted endorsement of Ford, but it was the best the outcast preacher could come up with under the circumstances.

Shortly thereafter, in one of the most overtelevised election nights on record, the nation said thanks, but no thanks, to Gerald Ford's offer to stay on another four years. James Earl Carter had campaigned himself from national anonymity in backward Georgia, to national prominence in equally backward Washington, D.C.

And Billy Graham set about the task of getting his Fuller brush–trained foot in the door of another administration.

9

Don't Call Us—
We'll Call You

When in doubt, tell the truth!
—MARK TWAIN

*I run scared all the time that I'll say
something or do something that will bring re-
proach to the Kingdom of God, and to the Church.*
—THE REVEREND WILLIAM F. GRAHAM

Every good Christian and Charlton Heston fan knows
that Moses brought the Ten Commandments down
from the mountain. For thousands of years they had
provided the rules to live by for millions of God-fearing
people.

But suppose Moses had returned to his people with
an extra commandment: "Thou shalt not make false,
ill-advised, hair-brained, or contradictory statements to
mass audiences, small groups, or the media."

If God had carved those words on a stone tablet,

217

hell would need a new annex just to handle the over-flow. And Billy Graham would have a tough time trying to get on the celestial elevator.

Billy is living proof that even a clever and cautious man has a hard time keeping his opinions to himself when someone shoves a microphone under his nose. The urge to say something—anything—is just too great, even though the words and thoughts can't stand the acid test of logic. Billy Graham is truly one of America's undisputed masters of saying the wrong thing at the wrong time. He hops through public life with one foot on the ground and the other in his mouth.

He's indeed lucky that Moses didn't stick the Israelites with a divine ban on wayward tonguewagging. But, what if he had? Would Billy be able to explain all those offending quotations and talk his way into heaven?

There's only one way to find out. Let's try to picture Billy's final judgment as Hollywood might portray it in one of those Claude Rains fantasies, like *Here Comes Mr. Jordan.*

The scene is set sometime in the future. Billy has just been notified that his mortal coil is about to be shuffled off. He's been permanently laid off in the middle of a Pittsburgh crusade and ordered to report at once to the heavenly relocation and employment office, for eternal reassignment.

The scene opens in Saint Peter's cloud-paneled executive suite. Billy is dressed in his best suit sitting nervously in front of the Great Gatekeeper's desk. Saint Peter thumbs through Billy's application for angelhood.

SAINT PETER: According to your application, you say you've just completed "a long and rewarding career on earth, preaching the Gospel, swaying millions with charisma and God's sweet, glorious message."

GRAHAM: Yes. I traveled the length and breadth of

the land, as Christ did, a humble servant, spreading the good word of. . . .

PETER: Uh . . . Reverend, with all due respect . . . lay back a little bit on the rhetoric and the imagery. One Billy Sunday around this place is enough. And frankly, plain talk makes the paperwork go a lot faster. Okay?

GRAHAM: I'm sorry. If it's a rule, I'll be glad to tone it down. Uh, to answer your question: Yes, I was an evangelist, and I had history's best convert record.

PETER: Now, I took the liberty of checking that claim with our bureau of statistics, and they confirmed it, so there's no need to fill out the good-works form today. We'll just skip it for now.

What I really want to do is get the details on some things you said outside the pulpit—all these citations on your record for violation of the Eleventh Commandment, article five, section C, of the Revised Holy Penal Code. There are several thousand complaints filed against you here.

GRAHAM: My secretary *always* paid my tickets—

PETER: I'm not talking about traffic violations. I'm talking about quotation violations. Like this one: In 1972 you told the *Dallas Times Herald,* "Good is getting better, but evil is getting worse." Now isn't that a bit contradictory?

GRAHAM: Well, I always had trouble taking definite stands on things. As I told that reporter from *People* magazine in Hong Kong, "I'm called upon to answer questions on every conceivable subject, and I feel unqualified."

PETER: Self-doubt is understandable, of course, Dr. Graham, but just try to relax and respond to *my* questions as best you can. I want to clear up a few discrepancies, so we can get your application moving.

For instance, our research department has attached

a note here. They say you always supported the right of free speech, except when Americans protested against the administration of another of our pending applicants —Richard M. Nixon, I think his name is.

GRAHAM: You mean that speech I made at Kansas State University? Let me make it perfectly clear, all I said was, "America reminds me of a mental institution where the patients have taken over and have locked up the doors."

PETER: Let's pursue this Nixon thing a bit further. It's my understanding that you stood by him, even though he disgraced himself and his country by getting involved in a criminal conspiracy called Watergate. A lot of people wanted to send him to jail, but you didn't. Why?

GRAHAM: Well, that depends on which magazine you read. I told *Harpers* that "Dick Nixon, I guess, is one of my ten best friends." That played nicely into my quote in *Christianity Today*: "When a friend is down, you don't go and kick him—you try to help him up."

PETER: Friendship's fine and a noble thing, Reverend, but doesn't God instruct us to steer clear of evil men and their evil ways?

GRAHAM: Oh yes, and I always took great care to preach that in my sermons. But you see, I don't think Dick Nixon was really evil. Oh sure, he used some bad judgment in Watergate, and I guess he must have trusted the wrong people. Now, I've got this clipping here from *People*: "In defending some of his friends, Nixon just got deeper and deeper. He didn't realize what was happening was actually breaking the law."

PETER: Reverend, correct me if I'm wrong, but didn't the Watergate hearings and other investigations definitely prove that Nixon knew he was doing something illegal but went ahead and did it anyway?

220

GRAHAM: Uh . . . yes, that did come to pass. But I was able to cover my tracks okay, by saying I deplored what Dick had done but had Christian compassion for him. I mean, if God can forgive people for sins, well, so can I, right?

PETER: I suppose you expressed all your charity to the media.

GRAHAM: Well, let's say I spoke when I was spoken to. I mean, I didn't go around begging reporters to ask me about it but, yes, I did call upon Americans to go easy on Dick because he had suffered enough already. When I talked to that guy from *Newsweek*, I even threw in Pat and Julie and Tricia, for good measure; "We should pray for Mr. Nixon and his family," I said, "as they seek privacy and rest. He has paid a terrible price for his mistakes; we should have compassion for him."

PETER: Don't get me wrong—I agree that compassion is a divine virtue. But did you have to suggest, as you did in *Christianity Today*, that Mr. Nixon maybe deserved another chance at public office?

GRAHAM: You mean when I said, "I'm sure if Mr. Nixon could redo many things, he would. I'm sure he's learned some very valuable lessons through this whole experience"?

PETER: Yes, that's the quote. Why did you say that?

GRAHAM: It's like I said in *People*, "I still have great affection for Nixon and great respect for him. Nixon can tell the total truth in the book he's writing. I think he will. But I could be wrong. I was wrong before."

PETER: I believe you also told *People*, "I never thought George Wallace was a real racist. He knew it was politically useful." Could you also have been wrong about that?

GRAHAM: Well, I gotta admit, there have been times I would like to have that quote back. Those newspapers and commentators didn't get my true meaning. You see, what I meant to say was—

PETER: That's okay, Reverend. Mr. Wallace is not one of our clients. I think we'd do better to move on to another topic that the front office is a little concerned about, the war in Vietnam. Frankly, we're a little upset over the fact that you supported President Johnson and President Nixon in their quest for total victory.

GRAHAM: You know, I still get angry when people say I was a hawk. I mean, I never liked war, and I always prayed that the fighting would stop and our boys could come home and all that. The Bible tells us that war is wrong, and I believe that.

PETER: Yes, we have all that on record—but we've also got this quote you gave to the *New York Times* in 1973. Unless we somehow got it wrong, you said, "We entered the war almost deliberately to lose it. You see, when the Russians went into Czechoslovakia, they went in with such overwhelming power that there was no battle. I don't think we should ever fight these long-drawn-out, half-hearted wars. It's like cutting a cat's tail off a half inch at a time."

GRAHAM: Are you asking me if I like animals? I do, you know—I came from a farm.

PETER: No, Reverend. The question is, were you saying we should have gone all out to clobber the enemy and win Vietnam decisively?

GRAHAM: Well, I wasn't the only one saying that in those days. I was just trying to make a point that if you *have* to go to war, you should get the misery over with as soon as possible.

PETER: Well, once the war was over you called it "a national tragedy." Why do you think it was?

GRAHAM: Oh, that's simple. As I always said, "If it hadn't been for the Vietnam war, Lyndon Johnson would really have done good things for America." Now, I hate to keep quoting from *People* magazine, but they did do a nice spread on me back in 1975. I have it here, if you'd like to see it.

PETER: Thank you for the offer, but it's already in our files.

GRAHAM: It was a five-and-a-half-page spread. Bob Dylan got only two pages in that very same issue. I even made the front cover and he didn't.

PETER: That's nice—but we really should press on here, Dr. Graham. I'd like to clear up some confusion about your statements on law and order.

GRAHAM: Ah, good. No confusion there. I always stood on the side of law and order. I only wish the Supreme Court had felt that way too.

PETER: Is it true that you were in favor of capital punishment, even though the Bible warns us, "Thou shalt not kill?"

GRAHAM: Well, I really had a rough time trying to work that one out. I remember in Atlanta—I think it was in 1973—a reporter asked me if I believed in the electric chair, and I said, "In the Bible, people were stoned to death for kidnapping, murder, fornication, adultery, and a number of crimes. I am sure no person today would say this is what we ought to do."

PETER: What you said in Atlanta doesn't seem to agree with what you told reporters in Johannesburg, South Africa, that very same year. Let me read your quote:

"I think where capital punishment is administered equally to black and white, it's been proven to be a deterrent. And if a rapist was castrated, that would stop him pretty quick!"

223

GRAHAM: Oh, brother—I was afraid that one might come up again. You gotta believe me when I say I wish I'd never mentioned that castration thing. I've spent years trying to explain that I didn't really mean it literally—it was just a figure of speech. You know, the kind of thing that plays big in South Africa and Betty Friedan rallies. I had no idea the remark would wind up on the Associated Press, worldwide.

PETER: While we're on law and order, I want to ask you about what you said right after the 1968 Democratic-convention violence. You were quoted saying something to the effect that you didn't blame the Chicago police for overreacting, because the protesters were so abusive to them.

GRAHAM: For sure—those radicals really made it rough on the officers. But don't get the idea that I just favored the Chicago police. I recall the time I addressed a group of New York's finest and told them, "Cops are God's personal agents for punishment." They really seemed to like that. There was lots of applause, and I got *invited back*!

PETER: I don't doubt it. By the way, let's back up to something you said. You used the term *radicals* in connection with the 1968 convention. You didn't much care for the protesters, did you?

GRAHAM: Oh no, that's not really true. Most of those kids were just disillusioned and misguided. I always made a point of saying that in youth seminars, and even at some crusades. My complaint was really with some of the protest leaders.

Were you at the Southern Baptist convention in 1970?

PETER: No. I was busy here.

GRAHAM: Well, that was the convention where I

really laid into those rabble rousers. I said, "Some of the radical groups in this country are being led by so-called clergymen. Where many of these men get the 'Reverend' in front of their names, I do not know. Certainly they don't get it from God!" Not bad, eh?

PETER: Not fair, might be a better way of putting it. Isn't it true that *you* never actually earned a doctorate, even though you call yourself *Dr.* Graham?

GRAHAM: Now, hold on there! I never accused any doctors of leading demonstrations!

PETER: The record shows that you once advised a British TV personality to stay out of America because of lawlessness and disorder there.

GRAHAM: Oh, you mean my good friend David Frost! Actually, I didn't tell him to stay out—just to be careful. I was on his show in London, and what I said was, "Only a handful of our mental patients are confined. Most mental patients are still on the outside, and they are after good people like you and me." By the way, I almost performed David's wedding ceremony, you know, but he got stood up at the altar.

PETER: Yes, he told me about that the last time he applied to us. But back to the point—I'm told you were terrified of being attacked by a madman or criminal or someone like that.

GRAHAM: Oh yes, all the time. That's why I once told a magazine reporter, "I get threatening letters which I turn over to the FBI, and they tell me which ones to consider seriously."

PETER: Well, when the FBI wasn't looking out for you, who did?

GRAHAM: My security people, of course. They took care of the guard fence and the dogs. But I'm not sure who put up that sign on my gate, though.

225

PETER: What sign was that?

GRAHAM: The one that said, "Trespassers will be eaten!"

PETER: Weren't you criticized for hiding away from the people you said you were trying to serve, what with bodyguards and warning signs and all?

GRAHAM: Well, no. The sign was really just supposed to be a joke, you know. That's how we explained it when a reporter spotted it and wrote one of those snotty stories I used to hate so much.

PETER: Suppose we get off that topic now and talk about sex.

GRAHAM: All right. I often discussed sex in my sermons, you know. I'll never forget the advice I gave to one audience of young people back in the sixties. "There is nothing wrong with sex. God gave it to us for certain reasons—for fulfillment, for communication, and for propagation. But *only* within the bonds of marriage."

PETER: Yes, we have a reprint of that sermon. Wasn't it the one where you told them not to feel guilty about having feelings of lust for the opposite sex?

GRAHAM: You liked that one, huh? Yes, I told those kids, "When temptation comes, accept the fact that it's normal to be tempted, that it's normal to have sex hunger."

PETER: If you truly believed that, why did you criticize 1976 presidential candidate Jimmy Carter for confessing to "mental" lust in *Playboy* magazine?

GRAHAM: Jerry Ford was running behind in the Gallup poll.

PETER: I see. Okay, Reverend, I think that will take care of our general questions.

GRAHAM: Oh, good. When do I get my wings? I take a 44 long.

226

PETER: Oh, no, we're not done with the processing procedure yet. We still have to go through the standard-quotation free-association test. It's simple. All I do is give you a topic, and you respond with the first documented quote that comes into your head.

GRAHAM: You mean I have to come up with something I really said in public?

PETER: That's right. Are you ready?

GRAHAM: Yes. But please hurry. I'm already late for my afternoon prayer with Ruth. We kneel and seek guidance several times a day, you know.

PETER: So I've heard. The first topic is transcendental meditation.

GRAHAM: "Transcendental meditation is evil, because when you are meditating, it opens space within you for the devil to enter."

PETER: The Equal Rights Amendment.

GRAHAM: "Women belong in the home. . . . Homosexuals are sick. . . . The whole thing bears looking into."

PETER: Actor John Wayne.

GRAHAM: "He's done as much for this country as Thomas Paine."

PETER: Contemporary music.

GRAHAM: "We need a whole lot more Jesus and a whole lot less rock and roll."

PETER: Pat Nixon's drinking.

GRAHAM: "What's wrong with a little cordial after dinner?"

PETER: "Mary Hartman, Mary Hartman."

GRAHAM: "Wicked, depraved, and a sure sign our society is going down the tube."

PETER: The TV prime-time family hour.

GRAHAM: "My family and I love to sit around and watch Cher, now that her navel's covered up."

PETER: *(making final notation on questionnaire):*
Let's see—I think that just about covers it, unless there is anything you want to add.

GRAHAM: Well, when I called your secretary, Miss Woods, she said that it might be a good idea to bring along a few quotes from other people—for references, I guess. So I took the liberty of putting together a few of my favorites. May I read them to you?

PETER: I suppose if Ruth can wait, so can I. Go ahead—you can read a few.

GRAHAM: Here's a nice one. Back in 1960 Dick Nixon was really in a campaign dogfight against John F. Kennedy. It was really important to him to win. But when I told Dick I was afraid to endorse him, he was really nice about it. He said, "Billy, your ministry is more important to me than my election to the presidency." I think that was the statement of a good Christian, don't you?

PETER *(looking at his hourglass):* Read the next one.

GRAHAM: Okay. When John Connally was governor of Texas, before that milk-scandal thing came up, he told an audience, "Billy Graham is more than a preacher, more than an evangelist, more than a Christian leader. In a greater sense, he has become our conscience." Isn't that a knockout—the conscience for a whole nation! Even Catholics and Jews.

PETER: Yes, that's certainly something to think about. Keep going, please.

GRAHAM: You're gonna love this one! Remember back in 1957, when I decided to have that big crusade in New York City and all the critics said I was wasting my time? Well, singer Ethel Waters really told them where to get off. She said, "God don't sponsor no flops!" Love that lady! She was a black person, you know.

PETER: Yes, Dr. Graham. I know that. She works in our heavenly host choral department.

GRAHAM: Then there's this nice quote from Spiro Agnew, just before he got in tax trouble—

PETER: Uh . . . Reverend, it's getting close to closing time, and I think you can just give me those references and I'll attach them to your file.

GRAHAM: But Ted said I was "not afraid to speak out for what's right in America and—"

PETER: Yes, yes, I'm sure he did. But really, Dr. Graham, there's no need to recite all these quotes. Our evaluation team can read them later.

GRAHAM: Okay. Well, thanks very much. When should I pick up my halo. I wear a six and seven-eighths.

PETER: (*brusquely*): We'll let you know. Just give your number to Rosemary on the way out.

GRAHAM: (*rising to shake hands*): Well, once again, thanks. I'm looking forward to working with you. And as I always used to say on the *Hour of Decision* radio show, May the Lord bless you real good!

(*Door closes.* PETER *picks up phone, dials extension 1.*)

PETER: Hello, chief? He's gone.

CHIEF: What did I tell you? Isn't he worse than Lyndon?

PETER: Tell me about it! What should I do with his application? You want me to process it or send it downstairs?

CHIEF: No, no—it wouldn't look good to turn him down now. Approve it, but do me a favor, will you?

PETER: Haven't I always?

CHIEF: Assign him to the evangelistic division and keep him on the road. I don't want him hanging around the office. We have enough trouble with reporters as it is.

229

A Benediction for Billy

*I know no way of judging the
future, than by the past.*
—PATRICK HENRY

Chances are the Pearly Gate showdown between
Graham and Saint Peter is still many years away. At
fifty-eight, Billy has slowed down a little as a result of
some illnesses and just plain years, but he has an ambitious decade of crusading mapped out for the rest of the
seventies and right into the eighties.

Despite bad lungs, prostate trouble, and phlebitis,
Billy appears indestructible, at least compared to
others.

President Truman, who booted him out of the

White House and called him a phony, is dead and gone. President Nixon, who praised Graham as "a friend and patriot," is washed up and living in exile. Mickey Cohen, who took several thousand dollars in exchange for faking Christianity and jazzing up a crusade, is also dead. Watergate is exhausted. The tear gas at the Billy Graham premiere at a Beverly Hills theater is gone with the wind. But the preacher keeps on preaching.

Billy has crusades planned in the South and the Midwest this next year and then goes overseas again.

The country-boy crusader will put on a one-week soul extravaganza in Asia's newest showcase dictatorship, the Republic of the Philippines. It is likely he won't find many converts among the fiercely Catholic and Muslim Filipinos, but he will enjoy the amenities at the Manila Intercontinental Hotel, plus the red-carpet treatment from President Ferdinand Marcos and his power-behind-the-throne first lady, Imelda.

While Billy mingles with the Marcos mob at Malacanang Palace, hundreds of political prisoners will continue to rot in rat-infested government dungeons, and the hard-won Philippine democracy will continue to smother under a blanket of martial law.

It is likely that the evangelist will not mention those conditions, since he will be hanging out with the government officials who created them. Billy Graham is always a good guest on foreign soil.

After the Philippines, Billy will seek a change of climate with a major crusade in Stockholm, Sweden. At this writing, the crusade-preparation team is working out the details in Minneapolis, but the basics are well in hand.

Billy will plead with the Swedes to turn to God, leave their porno shops, and find a better life. But recent surveys show that the Scandinavians have already begun a big swing from "anything goes" back to prudishness. Graham's visit is just a unique opportunity to jump on the bandwagon. If American tourists didn't frequent the sex shops that have made Stockholm so famous, the shops would go out of business—the Swedes are no longer very interested.

No matter where Billy Graham travels in the years ahead, only the locale, not the tactics, will change. The techniques are all time tested. The system works. Graham will gather all the souls and donations he can in his supersimplistic approach to salvation. As he once told David Frost on a British television show: "The average American has the intelligence of a twelve-year-old, religiously. And so I try to speak to everyone in a sense as though they are children when it comes to religion. And they listen."

Now Billy may be an incurable snob, talking down to the faithful, but his attitude is based on the oldest, soundest axiom in the Fuller brush salesmen's handbook. Get your foot in the door, keep the pitch simple, make your sale, get the cash, and get out fast. It's the only way to run your territory and keep your commissions growing.

But for all his successful sales skill, don't look for Billy to peddle himself to the newest residents in the White House. Although he may drag his sample case into the foyer from time to time in the years ahead, he will not be allowed to open it. President Jimmy Carter has never been in a buying mood, and it's unlikely he ever will be.

Carter is a self-contained, self-assured, Sunday-school-teachin' Southern Baptist who doesn't need any outside help with his spiritual life. Jimmy was "born again" years ago, and he says once is quite enough, thank you. Besides, his own sister is his favorite evangelist.

But there's a whole lot more to it than personal peace of mind and family loyalty. Newsmen who have covered President Carter since his early days in the Georgia legislature say he firmly believes that the best kind of Christian is the quiet Christian. He can't stand people who ballyhoo and breast beat in the name of the Lord—people like Billy Graham.

Carter likes his religion low-keyed and dignified, especially in the light of unfounded opposition campaign predictions that the election of a Southern Baptist to the presidency would mean the end of the church-state dividing line. Few people in this country know that Carter quietly fought to integrate his hometown church in Plains, Georgia, long before it became a Republican campaign issue in 1976. Jimmy confirms the story, but he doesn't publicize it, because it was a matter between him and the elders, not the public at large.

There's a third very important reason why Billy Graham won't be able to add Jimmy Carter to his president collection—politics. Billy was a thinly veiled Ford supporter in 1976, and everyone knew it. His attacks on Jimmy's *Playboy* sexual confessions were blatantly political and hopelessly misguided. (National polls ultimately showed that a majority of Americans disagreed with Graham and admired Carter for his courage in admitting he had feelings of temptation and lust.)

Billy's hopes of breaking into the Carter inner circle were permanently snuffed out shortly after election day, when he openly criticized the new president for allowing social drinkers to pursue their favorite vice within the executive mansion. It made a hit with the

WCTU, no doubt, but it all but guaranteed that Billy will have to spend the next four (or maybe eight) years on the outside of the administration, looking in with his nose pressed to the glass.

For the time being, he'll have to settle for those late-evening calls and occasional unpublicized side trips to San Clemente. Dick Nixon isn't president any more, but he still thinks and acts as if he is, and that seems to be good enough for Billy. After all, playing "let's pretend" can be fun, when there aren't any other, more realistic games tucked away in the toy box.

But don't bother to say any prayers for Billy Graham, just because he's got the cold shoulder from the nation's leading Baptist. The preacher's overall popularity and influence have never been broader or better. The growth curve on the boardroom wall at Billy Graham Evangelistic Association headquarters continues to go up.

Thanks to effective use of radio and television, the projections indicate Billy will be seen and heard by more and more people with every passing year. Right now, he reportedly has two more sure-fire bestselling books in the ghost-writing stage. *The Hour of Decision* radio show is sold out well in advance, tape-cassette sermons are being gobbled up faster than they can be made, and requests for personal, full-dress crusades are being turned down by the score every week.

Worldwide Pictures will continue to prosper and enjoy its tax breaks. This year alone, production of two more inspirational movies has got underway. One will tell the heart-tugging story of Kim Wickes, a blinded South Korean orphan who escaped drowning at the hands of her own misguided father and went to America to become a promising young singer.

The second color Graham feature will dramatically

recount the tragedy of Joni Eareckson. It's the tale of a happy, healthy teenage girl who wound up as a hopeless quadraplegic in a wheelchair, after breaking her neck in a Chesapeake Bay diving accident.

The stories of Joni and Kim are both true. Both will have identical scenarios once they hit the silver screen sometime next year: Girl battered by adversity; girl curses God; but girl finally sees light, accepts God's will, and builds new life"—Kim as a soprano, Joni as a highly acclaimed artist.

Like the folks down the street at Walt Disney Studios, Billy always insists on happy endings. And happy endings are what successful show business is all about. Leaving your audience down in the dumps is bad box office, whether you're a cartoon image on celluloid or a flesh-and blood image behind a pulpit.

But if you want the folks to keep on buying your tickets and coming back for more, all you gotta do is sell 'em the stuff that dreams are made of. Make 'em smile, give 'em fantasy, and send 'em back into the real world with a little bit of fairy-dusted hope in their hearts.

That's the simple formula for grabbing your share of the world's limelight and cashbox. It's made Mickey Mouse and Billy Graham what they are today:

. . . universally known.

. . . enduringly loved.

. . . unbelievably marketable.

. . . and two of Dick Nixon's favorite characters.

THE OFFICIAL BILLY GRAHAM
SCORE CARD

Year	City	Souls Allegedly Saved
1947	Grand Rapids, Mich.	500
	Charlotte, N.C.	1,200
1948	Augusta, Ga.	1,400
	Modesto, Calif.	not known
1949	Miami, Fla.	not known
	Baltimore, Md.	not known
	Altoona, Pa.	not known
	Los Angeles, Calif.	3,000
1950	Boston, Mass.	3,000
	Columbia, S.C.	12,000
	New England States	6,000
	Portland, Ore.	9,000
	Minneapolis, Minn.	5,700
	Atlanta, Ga.	8,000
1951	Southern States	not known
	Fort Worth, Tex.	4,000
	Shreveport, La.	5,446
	Memphis, Tenn.	4,698
	Seattle, Wash.	6,785
	Hollywood, Calif.	2,120
	Greensboro, N.C.	6,443
	Raleigh, N.C.	1,450
1952	Washington, D.C.	6,244
	American Cities Tour	not known
	Houston, Tex.	7,754
	Jackson, Miss.	5,927
	American Cities—Part II	not known
	Pittsburgh, Pa.	5,986
	Albuquerque, N.M.	3,011

Year	City	Souls Allegedly Saved
1953	Florida Cities	not known
	Chattanooga, Tenn.	4,406
	St. Louis, Mo.	3,065
	Dallas, Texas	5,869
	West Texas Tour	not known
	Syracuse, N.Y.	2,630
	Detroit, Mich.	6,980
	Asheville, N.C.	2,653
1954	West Coast Tour	2,650
	Nashville, Tenn.	9,067
	New Orleans, La.	4,932
1955	none	none
1956	Richmond, Va.	6,209
	Oklahoma City, Okla.	7,148
	Louisville, Ky.	6,870
1957	New York, N.Y.	61,148
1958	San Francisco, Calif.	28,898
	Sacramento, Calif.	4,965
	Fresno, Calif.	1,550
	Santa Barbara, Calif.	671
	Los Angeles, Calif.	2,117
	San Diego, Calif.	3,284
	San Antonio, Tex.	1,903
	Charlotte, N.C.	17,853
1959	Little Rock, Ark.	1,438
	Wheaton, Ill.	2,812
	Indianapolis, Ind.	9,320
1960	Washington, D.C.	4,971
	New York City	1,139
1961	Florida Cities Tour (15 cities)	14,015
	Upper Midwest Tour	7,233
	Philadelphia, Pa.	16,244

OFFICIAL BILLY GRAHAM SCORE CARD

Year	City	Souls Allegedly Saved
1962	Raleigh, N.C.	352
	Jacksonville, N.C.	426
	Chicago, Ill.	16,597
	Seattle, Wash.	609
	Fresno, Calif.	6,820
	Redstone Arsenal, Ala.	473
	El Paso, Tex.	3,821
1963	Los Angeles, Calif.	36,487
1964	Birmingham, Ala.	1,227
	Phoenix, Ariz.	4,239
	San Diego, Calif.	8,664
	Columbus, Ohio	12,149
	Omaha, Neb.	10,724
	Boston, Mass.	14,221
	Manchester, N.H.	500
	Portland, Me.	600
	Bangor, Me.	514
	Providence, R.I.	600
	Louisville, Ky.	860
1965	Hawaii Tour (4 cities)	3,000
	Dothan, Ala.	239
	Tuscaloosa, Ala.	not known
	Tuskegee Institute (Ala.)	not known
	Montgomery, Ala.	4,414
	Seattle, Wash.	not known
	Denver, Colo.	10,251
	Houston, Tex.	14,063
1966	Greenville, S.C.	7,311
1967	Kansas City, Mo.	11,379
1968	Portland, Ore.	7,950
	San Antonio, Tex.	4,326
	Pittsburgh, Pa.	12,414

Year	City	Souls Allegedly Saved
1969	New York City	10,852
	Anaheim, Calif.	20,336
1970	Knoxville, Tenn.	12,303
	New York City	6,025
	Baton Rouge. La.	9,076
1971	Lexington, Ky.	2,100
	Chicago, Ill.	11,889
	Oakland, Calif.	21,670
	Dallas-Ft. Worth, Tex.	12,830
1972	Charlotte, N.C.	4,709
	Birmingham, Ala.	9,788
	Cleveland, Ohio	19,608
1973	Atlanta, Ga.	9,735
	Minneapolis-St. Paul, Minn.	16,520
	Raleigh, N.C.	10,568
	St. Louis, Mo.	5,814
1974	Phoenix, Ariz.	9,718
	Los Angeles, Calif.	1,644
	Norfolk-Hampton, Va.	6,296
1975	Albuquerque, N.M.	8,657
	Jackson, Miss.	7,335
	Lubbock, Tex.	7,071
1976	Seattle, Wash.	18,136
	Williamsburg, Va.	514
	San Diego, Calif.	10,215
	Detroit, Mich.	14,039
1977	Still Saving	